smacaroons

arscrackers

onstriangles

eelssquares

ersbrownies

zelstruffles

the
cookie
book

Published by Fog City Press
814 Montgomery Street
San Francisco, CA 94133 USA

Copyright © 2001 Weldon Owen Pty Ltd
Reprinted 2002

Chief Executive Officer: John Owen
President: Terry Newell
Publisher: Lynn Humphries
Art Director: Kylie Mulquin
Editorial Manager: Janine Flew
Editorial Coordinator: Tracey Gibson
Production Manager: Martha Malic-Chavez
Business Manager: Emily Jahn
Vice President International Sales: Stuart Laurence

Project Editors: Janine Flew and Anna Scobie
Project Designer: Jacqueline Richards
Food Photography: Valerie Martin
Food Stylist: Sally Parker
Home Economist: Michelle Earl

ISBN 1 875137 95 5

Color reproduction by SC (Sang Choy) International Pte Ltd
Manufactured by Kyodo Printing Co. (S'pore) Pte Ltd
Printed in Singapore

A Weldon Owen Production

the
cookie
book

FOG CITY PRESS

contents

INTRODUCTION 6

PART ONE: RECIPES 8

chocolate and coffee 10

butter, spice, and honey 76

citrus 132

fruit 150

coconut 192

nuts 204

savory 260

PART TWO: TECHNIQUES   278

    making cookie dough   280

    measuring ingredients   282

    mixing cookie dough   284

    making drop cookies   286

    making bar cookies   288

    making cutout cookies   292

    making sliced cookies   294

    making shaped and molded cookies   296

    making pressed cookies   298

    toppings and meringues   300

    finishing touches   304

    storing cookies   307

GLOSSARY   308

INDEX   313

ACKNOWLEDGMENTS   320

crazy about cookies

No other kind of baking is as simple and informal as making cookies. Whether you are an experienced cookie baker or an enthusiastic novice, you will find inspiration in the pages that follow. The basic techniques demonstrated in Part Two will give you the skills to keep your cookie jar filled with the irresistible confections that appear throughout this book.

It is hard—sometimes it's almost impossible—to keep a cookie jar filled. No matter how many batches of buttery shortbread, craggy chocolate-dotted drop cookies, or elegant meringue kisses come out of the oven, they seem to disappear almost before they cool. And it isn't only little hands that reach for these delectable treats. Everyone succumbs to their fragrant allure.

In this collection of recipes you will find many that will evoke sweet memories of childhood favorites lovingly prepared in a kitchen perfumed with the warm smells of spices. Others will be entirely new, created to appeal to more sophisticated, grown-up tastes. All reflect years of combined culinary experience that ensures a successful result every time you bake.

The recipes are designed for cooks of all skill levels. Every important stage of cookie making, from measuring to mixing to shaping, plus all the professional tricks for decorating and finishing, is included. All the steps are explained in easy-to-understand language.

Part One presents over 140 recipes. As well as cookie recipes, there are recipes for finishing flourishes such as icings and toppings for cookies and delectable sauces for brownies. Part Two covers the basics, including how to store finished cookies properly to maintain their just-baked freshness, and how to achieve success with the various types of cookie: sliced, shaped, and molded cookies; pressed, or spritz; bar cookies; whimsical cutouts; and specialties such as French madeleines and Italian biscotti. Tips appear throughout the book, from basic equipment needs to recipe variations to helpful hints and a glossary of ingredients.

Consider this book your personal recipe file. Don't hesitate to make notes, if you need to, when variations come to mind. The recipes are so inventive and the directions so clearly explained that you just might create something new as you go along. Above all, enjoy the pleasures of home baking and the delicious creations that result.

part
One

recipes

chocolate and coffee

butter, spice, and honey

citrus ❖ fruit ❖ coconut

nuts ❖ savory

chocolate
and
coffee
cookies

chocolate chip
cookies

makes 24

1/2 cup (4 oz/125 g) butter or margarine

1/2 cup (3 1/3 oz/105 g) firmly packed brown sugar

1/2 cup (4 oz/125 g) superfine (caster) sugar

1 egg

1 teaspoon vanilla extract (essence)

1 3/4 cups (7 oz/220 g) self-rising flour

1/2 teaspoon salt

1 cup (6 oz/185 g) sweet (milk) chocolate chips

1/2 cup (2 1/2 oz/75 g) chopped nuts of your choice

❖ Preheat an oven to 375°F (190°C/Gas Mark 4). Lightly butter 2 baking sheets or line them with parchment (baking) paper.

❖ In a medium bowl, combine the butter or margarine and both of the sugars and, using an electric mixer on medium to high speed, cream until light and fluffy. Add the egg and vanilla and beat well. Sift together the flour and salt and add to the butter mixture. Mix until well combined. Stir in the chocolate chips and nuts.

❖ Place heaping teaspoonfuls on the prepared baking sheets, spacing them 2 inches (5 cm) apart. Bake for 12–15 minutes. Allow to cool on the baking sheets for 5 minutes, then transfer to wire racks to cool completely.

espresso meringue kisses

makes about 48

Espresso powder imparts a distinct coffee flavor to the meringue base of these soft, chewy, chocolate-drizzled confections.

2 egg whites

3/4 cup (6 oz/185 g) superfine (caster) sugar

1 teaspoon instant espresso coffee powder

1 teaspoon vanilla extract (essence)

CHOCOLATE GANACHE

1/3 cup (3 fl oz/80 ml) heavy (double) cream

2 teaspoons superfine (caster) sugar

2 teaspoons butter or margarine

3/4 cup (4 oz/125 g) semisweet (plain) chocolate, chopped

❖ Preheat an oven to 325°F (160°C/Gas Mark 3). Line 2 baking sheets with parchment (baking) paper or greaseproof paper.

❖ For the meringues, place the egg whites in a medium mixing bowl and let stand at room temperature for 30 minutes. Stir together the sugar and espresso powder. Add the vanilla to the egg whites. Beat with an electric mixer on medium speed until soft peaks with curling tips form when the beaters are lifted from the mixture. Gradually add the sugar–espresso powder mixture, 1 tablespoon at a time, beating on high speed until the sugar is almost dissolved and stiff peaks with straight tips form when the beaters are lifted from the mixture.

❖ Drop slightly heaping teaspoons of the mixture onto the prepared baking sheets, spacing them 2 inches (5 cm) apart. Bake for 15–20 minutes, or until lightly browned. Using a spatula, transfer to wire racks to cool.

❖ While the cookies are baking, make the chocolate ganache: In a heavy saucepan stir together the cream, sugar, and butter or margarine. Cook over medium-high heat, stirring, until the sugar is dissolved. Bring the mixture to a boil. Place the chocolate in a heatproof bowl and pour the boiling cream mixture over it. Let stand for 5 minutes, then stir until smooth. Drizzle meringues with chocolate ganache just before serving. (The ganache may be refrigerated for several days. When ready to use, reheat it in a small saucepan over low heat, stirring constantly, until it is smooth and of drizzling consistency.)

double chocolate cookies

makes about 40

These cookies will have have a more intense flavor if you use the best-quality chocolate you can find. Confectionery stores or gourmet food stores usually have a good selection.

¾ cup (6 oz/185 g) butter

1¼ cups (9 oz/280 g) brown sugar

3 eggs

1 teaspoon vanilla extract (essence)

1 cup (4 oz/125 g) plain flour

1½ cups (6 oz/185 g) self-rising flour

½ cup (1½ oz/45 g) unsweetened cocoa powder

1⅓ cups (8 oz/250 g) white chocolate chips

❖ Preheat an oven to 365°F (185°C/Gas Mark 4). Line a large baking sheet with parchment (baking) paper.

❖ In a large mixing bowl beat the butter with an electric mixer on medium speed for 30 seconds. Add the sugar; beat until creamy.

❖ Beat in the eggs, one at a time, until thoroughly mixed. Beat in the vanilla.

❖ Sift together the plain flour, self-rising flour, and cocoa powder into the butter mixture. Stir to combine. Fold in the white chocolate chips.

❖ Place level tablespoons of the mixture on the prepared baking sheet, spacing them well apart. Bake for 10–12 minutes. Let the cookies cool on the baking sheet for a few minutes before transferring them to a wire rack to cool completely.

recipe variation

If you like larger chunks of chocolate in your cookies, replace the chocolate chips with an equal amount of roughly chopped white or semisweet (plain) chocolate.

chocolate nut cookies

makes about 20

These cookies are just slightly chocolatey. Any kind of nuts can be used in them, either a single type or a combination. Roasted nuts will give the best flavor. See page 211 for information on how to roast your own.

2 tablespoons semisweet (plain) chocolate chips

3 tablespoons (1½ oz/45 g) butter or margarine

½ cup (4 oz/125 g) brown sugar

1 egg, lightly beaten

1¼ cups (5 oz/155 g) self-rising flour, sifted

¼ cup (1 oz/30 g) finely chopped nuts of your choice

½ cup (2 oz/60 g) confectioners' (icing) sugar, sifted, plus extra for sprinkling

❖ Preheat an oven to 375°F (190°C/Gas Mark 4). Lightly butter 2 baking sheets or line them with parchment (baking) paper.

❖ In a small saucepan over low heat, melt the chocolate and butter or margarine. Beat well until smooth. In a medium bowl, whisk together the sugar and egg until light and creamy. Beat in the chocolate mixture, then stir in the sifted flour and the nuts.

❖ Turn out onto a lightly floured surface and knead briefly to form a smooth dough. Wrap in plastic wrap and chill for 15 minutes.

❖ Divide the mixture into 20 portions, then form each into a ball and toss it in a little confectioners' sugar. Flatten the balls slightly and place them about 2 inches (5 cm) apart on the prepared baking sheets. Cook for 8–10 minutes. Leave to stand on the baking sheets for 5 minutes, then transfer to a wire rack to cool.

❖ Store in an airtight container for up to 1 week. If desired, sift a little confectioners' sugar over the cookies before serving.

chocolate salami

makes 3 rolls

This Mexican confection, with its chunks of cookies and walnuts, actually resembles a fat-flecked salami when it is sliced. It is ideal to give as a Christmas present or to offer to guests with coffee. The strong chocolate flavor and the aroma of the coffee liqueur make it a delicious treat.

1 cup (8 oz/250 g) sweet (unsalted) butter

5 oz (155 g) bittersweet chocolate, chopped

2 tablespoons unsweetened cocoa powder

¾ cup (6 oz/185 g) superfine (caster) sugar

5 eggs, lightly beaten

¼ cup (2 fl oz/60 ml) Kahlua or other coffee liqueur

1 teaspoon vanilla extract (essence)

3 packages (each 6½ oz/200 g) of any plain vanilla cookies, broken into small chunks

1 cup (4 oz/125 g) chopped walnuts

❖ Melt the butter in the top half of a double boiler over simmering water, then add the chocolate and allow it to melt. Add the cocoa and sugar and mix well. Remove from the heat. Gradually add the eggs, whisking to incorporate. Add the liqueur and vanilla and stir to combine. Allow the mixture to cool slightly.

❖ Fold the cookie chunks and nuts into the chocolate mixture. Place three 8 x 11-inch (22 x 30-cm) sheets of parchment (baking) paper or greaseproof paper onto a work surface. Spoon an equal amount of the cookie mixture onto each sheet of paper and roll tightly into a log, twisting the ends to seal.

❖ Place in the freezer immediately for about 3 hours or until frozen.

❖ While still frozen, finely slice (like salami), and serve. The rolls can be kept in the freezer for up to 4 months.

recipe**variations**

If desired, replace the purchased cookies with homemade ones of your choice. Try Sugar Cookies (page 77), unfilled Melting Moments (page 92), uniced Honey Snowflakes (page 98), Shortbread (page 108), or Ladyfingers (page 118).

Experiment with different liqueurs, such as Frangelico (hazelnut) or Cointreau or Grand Marnier (orange) in place of the Kahlua.

chocolate mint
sandwich cookies

makes 12

Chocolate and mint are a classic combination. The cool, fresh flavor of the mint essence complements the richness of the chocolate. These pastrylike cookies contain no butter. They look particularly pretty when made with a star-shaped cutter, but any other shape of cutter may be used.

½ cup (3 oz/90 g) semisweet (plain) chocolate or chocolate chips

1⅓ fl oz (40 ml) hot water

½ cup (2 oz/60 g) all-purpose (plain) flour

½ cup (2 oz/60 g) self-rising flour

¼ cup (1 oz/30 g) confectioners' (icing) sugar

1 large egg, beaten

PEPPERMINT FILLING

1 cup (4 oz/120 g) confectioners' (icing) sugar, sifted

1 teaspoon peppermint extract (essence)

1–2 tablespoons water

❖ Preheat an oven to 350°F (180°C/Gas Mark 4). Line a baking sheet with parchment (baking) paper or greaseproof paper.

❖ In the top half of a double boiler or in a heatproof bowl over a saucepan of simmering water, combine the chocolate and hot water and melt. Stir until smooth and combined, then allow to cool slightly.

❖ Sift together the plain flour, self-rising flour, and sugar. Combine the melted chocolate and beaten egg and pour over the flour mixture, stirring constantly with a wooden spoon to blend. The dough will be rather crumbly. Gather it into a ball by scooping and compressing the mixture with your hands, then wrap in plastic wrap and refrigerate for 15 minutes.

❖ Roll out the cookie dough between 2 pieces of parchment (baking) paper or waxed (greaseproof) paper to a thickness of ⅛ inch (3 mm). Using a 2-inch (5-cm) cutter, cut out shapes. Reroll any scraps and cut out more shapes. Place on the prepared baking sheet about 1 inch (2.5 cm) apart. Bake for 10 minutes. Transfer to a wire rack to cool.

❖ For the peppermint filling, combine the confectioners' sugar and peppermint. Gradually add enough water, a teaspoon at a time, to make a smooth paste. Place a little filling on one cookie and sandwich another cookie on top. Repeat until all are sandwiched.

chocolate kahlua truffle cookies

makes about 30

These no-bake cookies are quick, easy, and impressive, and almost any of your favorite liqueurs can be used to make them. Try hazelnut, orange, Irish cream, or chocolate flavors.

2½ cups (7½ oz/235 g) finely crushed chocolate wafers or plain cookie crumbs

1 cup (4 oz/125 g) finely chopped walnuts, pecans, pine nuts, almonds, or hazelnuts

1 cup (4 oz/125 g) sifted confectioners' (icing) sugar

⅓ cup (3 fl oz/80 ml) Kahlua or other liqueur

1–2 tablespoons water

⅔ cup (4 oz/125 g) semisweet (plain) chocolate, chopped

1 tablespoon solid vegetable shortening

1 cup (5 oz/150 g) chopped white chocolate

❖ In a large mixing bowl stir together the wafer or cookie crumbs, chopped nuts, confectioners' sugar, and Kahlua or other liqueur. Add just enough of the water so that the crumbs hold together. Shape the mixture into 1-inch (2.5-cm) balls. Place on a baking sheet lined with parchment (baking) paper.

❖ In a small, heavy saucepan over low heat, combine the semisweet (plain) chocolate and shortening and heat until melted. In another small, heavy saucepan heat the white chocolate over low heat until melted. With a fork, dip half the cookies into the dark chocolate mixture to coat; place on baking sheet. Dip remaining cookies in melted white chocolate to coat; place on baking sheet.

❖ With the tip of a spoon, thinly drizzle white chocolate mixture in a zigzag pattern over cookies coated with dark chocolate. Repeat with dark chocolate, drizzling over cookies coated with white chocolate. Refrigerate for about 30 minutes, or until chocolate is firm. Store in the refrigerator.

recipe hint

See pages 301–302 for information about melting and handling chocolate.

marshmallow
sandwich cookies

makes about 32

If marshmallow creme is unavailable, make the filling with 1⅓ cups (12 oz/375 g) cream cheese, ¾ cup (3 oz/90g) confectioners' sugar, and 1½ teaspoons vanilla extract (essence). Stir in nuts as directed below. For personalized cookies, write initials on each in chocolate.

⅓ cup (2 oz/60 g) semisweet (plain) chocolate, chopped

¾ cup (6 oz/185 g) butter or margarine, softened

¾ cup (6 oz/185 g) superfine (caster) sugar

1 teaspoon baking powder

1 egg

1 teaspoon vanilla extract

2½ cups (10 oz/315 g) all-purpose (plain) flour

FILLING

⅔ cup (6 oz/185 g) cream cheese, softened

1 cup (7 oz/220 g) marshmallow creme

½ cup (2 oz/60 g) finely chopped walnuts, pecans, or peanuts

DRIZZLE (OPTIONAL)

½ cup (3 oz/90 g) semisweet (plain) chocolate or white chocolate, chopped

1 teaspoon solid vegetable shortening

❖ Preheat an oven to 375°F (190°C/Gas Mark 4).

❖ For cookies, in a small, heavy saucepan, melt the chocolate over low heat, stirring constantly. Set aside. In a large mixing bowl, beat the butter or margarine with an electric mixer on medium to high speed for 30 seconds. Add the sugar and baking powder; beat until combined. Beat in the melted chocolate, egg, and vanilla. Beat in as much of the flour as you can with the mixer. Stir in any remaining flour with a wooden spoon. Shape dough into two 7-inch (18-cm) rolls. Wrap in greaseproof paper or plastic wrap. Chill dough for 2 hours, or until firm.

❖ Cut the rolls into slices a little less than ¼ inch (6 mm) thick. Place about 2 inches (5 cm) apart on ungreased baking sheets. Bake for 8–10 minutes, or until the edges are firm and the bottoms are lightly browned. Remove with a spatula and transfer to a wire rack to cool.

❖ Meanwhile, for filling, in a mixing bowl beat the cream cheese and marshmallow creme (or ingredients for alternative filling on page 24) with an electric mixer on medium speed until blended. Stir in the nuts. Spread about 2 teaspoons of filling on the bottoms of half of the cookies; top with the remaining cookies.

❖ If desired, for drizzle, in a small, heavy saucepan melt chocolate and shortening over low heat. Drizzle over tops of cookies. Cover the cookies and store in the refrigerator.

chocolate peppermint slices

makes about 30

If everyone is tired of plain old sugar cookies, make this delightful variation instead, in which different-colored layers of dough are stacked then cut, producing a novel striped effect. You can make the peppermint dough any color you like just by adding a few drops of food coloring.

1/2 cup (4 oz/125 g) butter or margarine

1/3 cup (3 oz/90 g) superfine (caster) sugar

1/4 teaspoon baking powder

1 cup (4 oz/125 g) all-purpose (plain) flour

1 oz (30 g) semisweet (plain) chocolate, melted and cooled

1/4 teaspoon peppermint extract (essence)

several drops food coloring (optional)

❖ Preheat an oven to 375°F (190°C/Gas Mark 4).

❖ In a medium mixing bowl beat the butter or margarine with an electric mixer on medium to high speed for 30 seconds. Add the sugar and baking powder; beat until combined. Beat in as much of the flour as you can with the mixer. Stir in any remaining flour with a wooden spoon. Divide the dough in half.

❖ Place half the dough in a small bowl. Stir in the melted chocolate, then knead the dough until it is uniformly chocolate-colored and not streaky.

❖ Add peppermint extract and, if desired, food coloring to the remaining dough and knead to distribute evenly. Make sure they are well mixed into all of the dough. Shape each half of dough into a log about 4 inches (10 cm) long. Wrap in greaseproof paper or plastic wrap. Chill for 2 hours, or until firm.

❖ On a lightly floured surface, roll and/or pat each log into a 6 x 3-inch (15 x 7.5-cm) rectangle. Cut each rectangle in half lengthwise, forming two 6 x 1½-inch (15 x 4-cm) rectangles. Stack all 4 rectangles on top of each other, alternating chocolate with peppermint dough. Press down lightly. Cut the stacked layers into ¼-inch (6-mm) thick slices. Place slices about 1 inch (2.5 cm) apart on ungreased baking sheets.

❖ Bake for 8–10 minutes, or until bottoms of cookies are a light golden brown. Remove with a spatula and transfer to a wire rack to cool.

cooking cookies in the
microwave oven

Cookies and bar cookies (slices) cook well in the microwave; however, fairly dry mixtures are the most successful. Cookies should be cooked on a microwave-safe baking tray or plate that has been covered with baking paper. Cook only about six cookies at a time, well spaced around the oven tray or plate. Be on the lookout for the appearance of brown spots on the cookies; these indicate overcooking. Cookies with a high concentration of sugar and those containing chocolate pieces and dried fruits are particularly susceptible, as these ingredients help generate excessive heat.

When cooking bar cookies, shield the corners of the baking pan with strips of aluminum foil to prevent these areas from overcooking. Remove the foil after half the cooking time. Lining the pan with parchment (baking) paper will assist in the removal of the bar cookies once they are cooked. Bar cookies usually need to be cooled in the pan, and sometimes chilled for 30 minutes, before being cut.

When making bar cookies that include packaged cereals and coconut among the ingredients, always press the dough down firmly before cooking, otherwise they tend to crumble when cut.

It is difficult to be precise in giving cooking times for microwave ovens, as individual ovens vary. The golden rule is to undercook the food, then check to see if it is done and return it to the oven if necessary. If it is almost cooked, any further cooking should be done in bursts of a few seconds only to avoid overcooking.

The recipes in this book are designed for a 650-watt oven. Ovens with less power will need a little more time and those with more power less time. The table, right, will serve as a quick reference. If in doubt, always be guided by your oven's instruction manual.

microwave timing

Power	Change of Timing per Minute (+ or −)
900 watts	− 40 seconds
850 watts	− 30 seconds
800 watts	− 20 seconds
750 watts	− 10 seconds
700 watts	− 5 seconds
650 watts	no change
600 watts	+ 5 seconds
550 watts	+ 10 seconds
500 watts	+ 20 seconds
450 watts	+ 30 seconds

microwave
chocolate
caramel
slice

makes 25

This lusciously sweet, sticky treat is a family favorite. In warm weather, store it in an airtight container in the refrigerator, where it will keep for several days. This recipe is designed for a 650-watt microwave oven: if your oven has a different wattage, see page 29 for conversions.

1/2 cup (3 1/2 oz/105 g) firmly packed brown sugar

1 cup (4 oz/125 g) self-rising flour, sifted

1 cup (3 oz/90 g) grated dried (desiccated) coconut

1/2 cup (4 oz/125) g butter, melted

CARAMEL FILLING

13-oz (410-g) can sweetened condensed milk

2 tablespoons light molasses or golden syrup

1 oz (30 g) butter, melted

CHOCOLATE TOPPING

125 g (4 oz) semisweet (plain) chocolate, chopped

1 1/2 oz (45 g) butter or solid vegetable shortening

❖ Line the base of a 9-inch (23-cm) square, shallow, microwave-safe casserole with parchment (baking) paper. Combine the brown sugar, flour, coconut, and melted butter in a bowl and mix well. (The mixture will be quite crumbly.) With the back of a spoon, press the mixture firmly and evenly into the casserole. Cook on high (100%) for 5–5½ minutes. The mixture should still feel a little soft but not damp. Cover lightly with a clean kitchen towel and let stand in the casserole until cool. If the base is not firm after standing, cook for 1 minute further on high.

❖ To make the caramel filling, combine the condensed milk, golden syrup, and butter in a microwave-safe bowl. Heat on high for approximately 7 minutes, stirring every minute for the first 3 or 4 minutes, then every 30 seconds until the mixture is a light caramel color and appears to have curdled. (When this happens, beat the mixture well to return it to a smooth consistency.) Test the caramel by placing 2 teaspoons of the mixture on a saucer and chill in the refrigerator for a few minutes. When it is firm enough to be cut with a knife without the mixture running together again, the caramel is ready. Pour the caramel over the base and spread evenly.

❖ To make the chocolate topping, combine the chocolate and vegetable shortening or butter in a microwave-safe bowl and melt on high for about 1 minute, stirring every few seconds. When it is melted, pour the mixture over the caramel. Let stand until firm enough to cut into slices. (If the day is warm, it may need to be chilled in the refrigerator for 30–60 minutes before cutting.) Cut into 25 pieces.

microwave chocolate fudge brownies

makes 30–35

When you're short on time but longing for a brownie, try this super-quick microwave version. This recipe is designed for a 650-watt microwave oven; if your oven uses a different wattage, see page 29 for conversions.

6 oz (185 g) semisweet (dark) chocolate

½ cup (4 oz/125 g) butter

¾ cup (5 oz/155 g) superfine (caster) sugar

2 eggs, lightly beaten

1 cup (4 oz/125 g) chopped pecans or walnuts

1½ cups (6 oz/185 g) all-purpose (plain) flour

❖ Line a 9-inch (23-cm) square microwave-safe pan with parchment (baking) paper.

❖ Break the chocolate into pieces and combine with the butter in a large microwave-safe bowl. Melt on high (100%) for 1½ minutes, or until almost melted, stirring every 30 seconds. Leave to stand for 1–2 minutes, during which time the chocolate should have melted completely. Stir in the sugar and then the eggs, a little at a time, beating well with a wooden spoon between each addition. Stir in the nuts and flour and pour into the prepared pan. Cook on high for 6–7 minutes until the center is just cooked when tested with a skewer.

❖ Transfer to a wire rack and allow to cool in the pan. When completely cool, chill for at least 30 minutes before cutting. Store in an airtight container.

recipe hint

See page 28 for hints on how to cook brownies in the microwave.

Chopped raisins or golden raisins (sultanas) may be substituted for the nuts.

apricot cream cheese chocolate brownies

makes 16

APRICOT CREAM CHEESE

3/4 cup (3 oz/90 g) dried apricots, chopped

3 tablespoons brandy

5 oz (155 g) cream cheese

2 tablespoons (1 oz/30 g) sweet (unsalted) butter

1/4 cup (2 oz/60 g) granulated (white) sugar

1 egg

BROWNIES

3 1/2 tablespoons (1 3/4 oz/50 g) sweet (unsalted) butter

2/3 cup (4 oz/125 g) semisweet (dark) chocolate

2 eggs

3/4 cup (6 oz/180 g) granulated (white) sugar

1 teaspoon vanilla extract (essence)

1 cup (4 oz/125 g) all-purpose (plain) flour

1/2 teaspoon baking powder

1/4 teaspoon salt

1/2 cup (2 oz/60 g) chopped walnuts

Whipped cream or ice cream, for serving

❖ Preheat an oven to 350°F (180°C/Gas Mark 4). Lightly butter an 8-inch (20-cm) square cake pan.

❖ For the apricot cream cheese, place the dried apricots in a bowl and pour over the brandy. Allow to stand for at least 1 hour.

❖ Beat the cream cheese and butter until smooth. Gradually add the sugar and continue beating until creamy. Add the egg and beat to combine. Stir in the apricots and brandy.

❖ For the brownies, heat the butter over low heat. When half melted, add the chocolate, broken into pieces, and stir to combine. When the chocolate is melted, remove from the heat and set aside.

❖ Beat the eggs until light and foamy. Gradually add the sugar and beat until pale and thickened. Fold in the chocolate-and-butter mixture, vanilla, sifted dry ingredients, and walnuts. Pour two-thirds of the mixture into the prepared pan. Pour the apricot cream cheese on top, then add the remaining chocolate mixture in spoonfuls. Using a skewer, swirl the apricot cream cheese through the chocolate mixture.

❖ Bake until a skewer inserted into the middle of the cake comes out barely moist, 35–40 minutes. Cool completely in the pan before turning out and slicing into 16 pieces.

❖ Serve with whipped cream or ice cream.

makes about 48

CRUST

2 cups (8 oz/250 g) all-purpose
(plain) flour

1/2 cup (2 oz/60 g) sifted
confectioners' (icing) sugar

1/2 teaspoon salt

3/4 cup (6 oz/185 g) cold butter

1–2 tablespoons cold water

FILLING

2 eggs, lightly beaten

1/2 cup (3 1/2 oz/105 g) packed
brown sugar

1 cup (4 oz/125 g) chopped pecans

1/2 cup (4 fl oz/125 ml) honey

1/4 cup (2 oz/60 g) butter, melted

2 tablespoons light (single) cream

1 teaspoon instant coffee
granules

1 teaspoon vanilla extract
(essence)

❖ Preheat oven to 350°F (180°C/Gas Mark 4). Line the base and sides of a 12 x 8 x 1-inch (30 x 20 x 2.5-cm) baking pan with a sheet of parchment (baking) paper, cutting into the corners of the paper to make it fit.

❖ For crust, sift together flour, confectioners' sugar, and salt into a bowl. Cut in the butter, or process in a food processor using the pulse button, until the mixture is crumbly. Gradually add enough cold water to bring the mixture together into a dough. Press evenly into base of prepared pan. Bake for 10 minutes.

❖ For filling, in another bowl stir together the eggs, brown sugar, pecans, honey, and melted butter. In a small bowl, stir together the cream, coffee, and vanilla until the coffee dissolves. Stir into the pecan mixture and spread evenly over the hot crust.

❖ Bake for 20 minutes, or until set. Cool in the pan on a wire rack. When cool, cut into squares, then cut each square into 2 triangles.

coffee-pecan
triangles

pecan fudge brownies

makes about 30

½ cup (4 oz/125 g) butter, chopped

200 g unsweetened (plain) chocolate, chopped

3 eggs

1½ cups (10½ oz/330 g) superfine (caster) sugar

1 teaspoon vanilla extract (essence)

1½ cups (6 oz/180 g) all-purpose (plain) flour

⅓ cup (1 oz/30 g) unsweetened cocoa powder

1½ cups (6 oz/180 g) chopped pecans

❖ Preheat an oven to 350°F (180°C/Gas Mark 4). Line the base and the 2 long sides of an 8 x 12-inch (20 x 30-cm) baking pan with parchment (baking) paper, extending it about 1 inch (2.5 cm) above the rim of the pan. This helps remove the cooked brownies from the pan.

❖ In a saucepan over low heat, melt the chopped butter and chocolate until just melted and combined. Remove from the heat and cool for 10 minutes.

❖ In a large bowl, using an electric mixer set on medium speed, beat together the eggs, sugar, and vanilla until the mixture is thick and creamy, about 3 minutes.

❖ Pour the butter and chocolate mixture into the egg mixture and fold in with a metal spoon until just combined. Fold in the sifted flour and cocoa, then the nuts, stirring until smoothly combined.

❖ Pour the batter into the prepared pan and spread evenly. Bake until firm, about 30 minutes.

❖ Transfer to a wire rack and let cool in the pan, then cut into slices.

chocolate-dipped
mushrooms

makes about 55

3 egg whites

½ teaspoon vanilla extract (essence)

¼ teaspoon cream of tartar

¾ cup (6 oz/185 g) granulated (white) sugar

⅔ cup (4 oz/125 g) semisweet (plain) chocolate, chopped

2 tablespoons sifted confectioners' (icing) sugar

2 teaspoons unsweetened cocoa powder

❖ Preheat an oven to 300°F (150°C/Gas Mark 2). Line 2 baking sheets with parchment (baking) paper or greaseproof paper. Set aside. Place the egg whites in a medium mixing bowl and let stand at room temperature for 30 minutes.

❖ Add the vanilla and cream of tartar to the egg whites. Beat with an electric mixer on medium speed until soft peaks form (tips curl when beaters are lifted out of the mixture). Gradually add the sugar, 1 tablespoon at a time, beating on high speed until very stiff peaks form (tips stand straight when beaters are lifted out of the mixture) and the sugar is almost dissolved. Spoon the mixture into a piping bag fitted with a large round nozzle (½-inch/12-mm opening). Pipe about two-thirds of the meringue mixture into 1½-inch (4-cm) diameter mounds about 1 inch (2.5 cm) apart on the prepared baking sheets. With the remaining meringue, pipe 1-inch (2.5-cm) tall bases about ½ inch (12 mm) apart on the baking sheets. (To get an even number of caps and stems, pipe caps and stems alternately until all the meringue is used up.)

❖ Bake for 20–25 minutes, or until the meringues just begin to brown. Turn off the oven. Let the meringues dry in the oven with the door closed for 30 minutes. Remove meringues from pans and transfer to a wire rack to cool.

❖ In a small, heavy saucepan over low heat, melt the chocolate. Spread a scant ½ teaspoon of the melted chocolate on the underside of each mushroom cap. Attach stems by pressing top ends in the center of the chocolate mixture, pressing gently into the mushroom cap. Let mushrooms dry upside down on racks until the chocolate is set. To serve, sift combined confectioners' sugar and cocoa powder over tops of mushrooms.

chocolate pistachio sandwich cookies

makes about 32

1 cup (8 oz/250 g) butter or margarine, softened

¾ cup (6 oz/185 g) granulated (white) sugar

¼ cup (2 oz/60 g) packed brown sugar

⅓ cup (1 oz/30 g) unsweetened cocoa powder

1 teaspoon baking powder

¼ teaspoon ground nutmeg

1 egg

1½ teaspoons vanilla extract (essence)

2 cups (8 oz/250 g) all-purpose (plain) flour

⅔ cup (3½ oz/80 g) ground pistachios, almonds, or pecans

FILLING

¼ cup (2 oz/60 g) butter or margarine, softened

¼ cup (¾ oz/20 g) unsweetened cocoa powder, sifted

2 cups (8 oz/250 g) confectioners' (icing) sugar, sifted

2 tablespoons milk

¾ teaspoon vanilla extract (essence)

extra milk (if required)

❖ Preheat an oven to 375°F (190°C/Gas Mark 4).

❖ In a large mixing bowl beat the butter or margarine with an electric mixer on medium to high speed for 30 seconds. Add the granulated sugar, brown sugar, cocoa powder, baking powder, and nutmeg; beat until combined. Beat in the egg and vanilla. Beat in as much of the flour as you can with the mixer. Stir in any remaining flour with a wooden spoon. Divide the dough in half. Cover and chill for 30 minutes, or until it can be shaped into rolls. Shape dough into two 8-inch (20-cm) rolls. Roll in ground nuts to coat. Wrap in plastic wrap and chill for 2 hours.

❖ Cut the dough into ¼-inch (6-mm) thick slices. Place the slices 2 inches (5 cm) apart on ungreased baking sheets. Bake for 8–10 minutes, or until edges are firm. Remove cookies from the baking sheets and transfer to a wire rack to cool.

❖ For the filling, in a bowl beat the butter or margarine until fluffy. Beat in the cocoa powder. Gradually add 1 cup (about 4 oz/125 g) of the confectioners' sugar, beating well. Slowly beat in the milk and vanilla. Gradually beat in the remaining confectioners' sugar. Beat in additional milk, if needed, to make a mixture of spreading consistency. Spread 1–2 teaspoons of the filling over the bottoms of half the cookies; top with remaining cookies, bottom sides down.

chocolate-cherry
parson's hats

makes about 30

¾ cup (6 oz/185 g)
butter, softened

¾ cup (6 oz/185 g)
granulated (white)
sugar

⅓ cup (1 oz/30 g)
unsweetened cocoa
powder

½ teaspoon baking
powder

1 egg

¼ teaspoon almond
extract (essence)

2 cups (8 oz/250 g)
all-purpose (plain) flour

30 maraschino (glacé)
cherries or ½ cup
(4 fl oz/125 ml)
cherry jam

1½ oz (45 g) white
chocolate

1 teaspoon solid
vegetable shortening

❖ Preheat an oven to 350°F (180°C/Gas Mark 4).

❖ In a mixing bowl beat the butter with an electric mixer on medium to high speed for 30 seconds. Add the sugar, cocoa powder, and baking powder; beat until combined. Beat in the egg and almond extract. Beat in as much of the flour as you can with the mixer. Stir in any remaining flour with a wooden spoon. Cover and chill for 3 hours, or until the dough is easy to handle.

❖ On a lightly floured surface, roll out the dough to a ¼-inch (6-mm) thickness. Using a 2½-inch (6-cm) round cutter, cut out rounds. Place a cherry or 1 teaspoon of the cherry jam onto the center of each round.

❖ To form each three-cornered hat, lift up 3 edges of each dough round. Fold the edges toward, but not over, the filling. Then pinch the 3 outer points together. Place cookies 2 inches (5 cm) apart on ungreased baking sheets. Refrigerate for 30 minutes to firm the dough.

❖ Bake for 10–12 minutes, or until the edges of the cookies are firm. Transfer to a wire rack to cool.

❖ In a small, heavy saucepan, melt the white chocolate and shortening over low heat; drizzle over cookies.

choosing chocolate

The botanical name for the cocoa tree, *Theobroma cacao*, means "food of the gods"; the world's many chocaholics would surely think this fitting.

Chocolate's flavor comes from cocoa solids (also known as cocoa mass), a paste made from fermented, dried, roasted, and ground cocoa beans. Sugar, cocoa butter, and flavorings are added to this paste, which is then blended and "conched," or kneaded. This process is lengthy and expensive but necessary for the best texture and flavor. Buy the best chocolate you can afford; the results are worth the small extra cost.

The best type of chocolate to use in cooking is semisweet (plain or dark), unless the recipe specifies otherwise. Semisweet chocolate contains a minimum 43 percent cocoa solids, but the best results will be obtained with a type containing at least 50 percent cocoa solids. Types containing up to 70 percent cocoa solids are available.

Unless specifically called for, avoid using milk chocolate in cooking, and do not substitute it for semisweet (plain) chocolate. The flavor of the dish will be affected, as milk chocolate has a lower percentage of cocoa solids. It is also often harder to work with, and is more sensitive to heat.

White chocolate is not true chocolate, as it contains no cocoa solids, only cocoa butter (or, in cheaper varieties, vegetable fat), milk, and sugar. It is sensitive to heat and hard to handle.

Never use "compound" chocolate; this is cheaper than other types of chocolate but has a greatly inferior taste and texture.

chocolate raspberry
brownies

makes 16

**Raspberry and chocolate
are a classic combination,
but other flavors of jam
or preserves, such as cherry
or plum, are equally luscious
in this recipe.**

1/2 cup (4 oz/125 g) butter or margarine

1/3 cup (2 oz/60 g) unsweetened (bitter) chocolate,
chopped

1 cup (8 oz/250 g) superfine (caster) sugar

2 eggs, lightly beaten

1 teaspoon vanilla extract (essence)

1/2 teaspoon almond extract (essence)

1 1/4 cups (5 oz/155 g) all-purpose (plain) flour

1/3 cup (3 oz/80 g) seedless raspberry jam or preserves

COCOA FROSTING

1 1/2 cups (6 oz/185 g) confectioners' (icing) sugar, sifted

3 tablespoons unsweetened cocoa powder, sifted

3 tablespoons (1 1/2 oz/45 g) butter, melted

1 teaspoon vanilla extract (essence)

1–2 tablespoons boiling water

chocolate raspberry brownies

❖ Preheat an oven to 350°F (180°C/Gas Mark 4). Butter an 8 x 8 x 2-inch (20 x 20 x 5-cm) baking pan and line the base and sides with parchment (baking) paper.

❖ For the brownies, in a medium saucepan melt the butter or margarine and chocolate over low heat, stirring frequently. Remove from the heat. Lightly whisk in the sugar, eggs, vanilla, and almond extract. Using a wooden spoon, lightly beat in the flour just until combined. (Do not overbeat or the brownies will fall when baked.)

❖ Spread the batter into the prepared baking pan. Spoon the jam in dollops at even intervals over the batter. Insert a small metal spatula or knife in the center of one spoonful of jam or preserves. Drag it through the jam and batter with a swirling motion until you reach another dollop of jam. Continue swirling the remaining jam to create a marble pattern.

❖ Bake for about 35 minutes, or until set. Transfer the pan to a wire rack and let the brownies cool in the pan.

❖ Meanwhile, for the cocoa frosting, in a medium mixing bowl stir together the confectioners' sugar, cocoa powder, melted butter, and vanilla. Gradually stir in enough of the boiling water to make a frosting of spreading consistency. Spread the frosting evenly over the entire surface of the brownies. If desired, score the frosting: Using just enough pressure to make score marks, pull the tines of a fork through the frosting on the diagonal. Cut into 16 squares. Store in an airtight container.

raspberry sauce

**makes 1½ cups
(12 fl oz/375 ml)**

1 cup (8 oz/250 g) fresh or thawed frozen raspberries

¼ cup (2 oz/60 g) granulated (white) sugar

1 tablespoon fruit-flavored liqueur (optional)

**Pour this simple sauce
over chocolate or fruit-
flavored brownies for a
quick but delectable
dessert. The liqueur
adds a touch of luxury;
try Kirsch or a peach
liqueur to bring out
the flavor of the
raspberries.**

❖ In a food processor, combine the raspberries and sugar
and process to a purée. Taste; add more sugar if necessary.
Strain the purée through a fine-mesh sieve to remove the
seeds. Add the fruit liqueur, if desired. Serve immediately or
cover and refrigerate for up to 3 days.

microwave sauces

These recipes are designed for a 650-watt microwave oven. If your oven uses a different wattage, see page 29 for conversions.

microwave brandy sauce

2 tablespoons cornstarch (cornflour)
1½ cups (12 fl oz/375 ml) milk
1 tablespoon (½ oz/15 g) butter
1 tablespoon granulated (white) sugar
¼ cup (2 fl oz/60 ml) brandy

❖ In a 1-quart (1-l) microwave-safe jug, combine the cornstarch and a little of the milk and mix to a smooth paste. Stir in the remaining milk, the butter, and sugar. Cook on high (100%) for 2 minutes. Stir, breaking up any lumps, then cook for 1–2 minutes more. Stir in the brandy. Serve hot.

makes about 2 cups (16 fl oz/500 ml)

microwave fudge sauce

¼ cup (2 oz/60 g) butter
30 g (1 oz) cooking chocolate
1½ cups (12 oz/375 g) granulated (white) sugar
¾ cup (6 fl oz/185 ml) evaporated milk
1 teaspoon vanilla extract (essence) or brandy

❖ Combine the butter and chocolate in a microwave-safe dish and cook on high (100%) for 1 minute. Stir, then cook for a further 30 seconds to 1 minute. Add the sugar, stir well, then add the evaporated milk. Cook on high for 2 minutes, stirring once. Continue to cook for 2–3 minutes more. Add the vanilla and brandy and stir well. Serve hot or warm. Store at room temperature.

makes about 2½ cups

blonde
brownies

makes 18

These are "Blondies", with
a melted chocolate and
toasted nut topping. Leave
the skin on the nuts and
chop them coarsely to add
visual appeal and crunch.

1½ cups (11½ oz/360 g) lightly packed brown sugar

⅔ cup (5 oz/155 g) butter or margarine

2 eggs

1½ teaspoons vanilla extract

1½ cups (6 oz/185 g) all-purpose (plain) flour

1 teaspoon baking powder

¾ teaspoon baking soda (bicarbonate of soda)

1 cup (6 oz/185 g) semisweet (plain) chocolate, chopped

⅔ cup (4 oz/125 g) toasted chopped hazelnuts or almonds

blonde brownies

❖ Preheat an oven to 350°F (180°C/Gas Mark 4).
Butter a 12 x 8 x 2-inch (30 x 20 x 5-cm) baking pan.

❖ In a bowl combine the brown sugar and butter and,
using an electric mixer, beat on medium to high speed
until light and fluffy. Add the eggs, one at a time,
stirring after each addition. Add the vanilla. Beat lightly
with a wooden spoon until just combined.

❖ Sift together the flour, baking powder, and baking
soda, then stir into the butter-and-sugar mixture.

❖ Pour the batter into the prepared pan and spread it
evenly. Sprinkle with the chopped chocolate and nuts.

❖ Bake for 35–40 minutes. Cut into 18 bars while still
warm; let bars cool completely in pan.

serving suggestion

If you're feeling self-
indulgent, these brownies
make a fantastic sundae
when topped with ice cream,
a sauce (see recipes in boxes
on pages 50 and 53), and
some extra chopped nuts.
Garnish with fresh fruit.

simply superb sauces

caramel sauce

1 cup (7 oz/220 g) packed brown sugar

1 cup (8 fl oz/250 ml) heavy (double) cream

6½ oz (200 g) sweet (unsalted) butter

❖ In a small saucepan over low heat, combine the sugar, cream, and butter. Stir until the sugar dissolves and the butter melts. Continue to stir for another 3 minutes, until well combined and warm. Serve immediately or cover and refrigerate for up to 2 days. Reheat gently before serving.

makes 2½ cups (20 fl oz/625 ml)

chocolate cream sauce

1 cup (8 fl oz/250 ml) heavy (double) cream

6½ oz (200 g) semisweet (plain) chocolate, broken into pieces

❖ Place the cream in a medium saucepan and bring to a boil, stirring gently to prevent scorching. Remove from the heat and stir in the chocolate. Let stand for 10 minutes, then stir until smooth. Serve immediately or cover and refrigerate for up to 2 days. If desired, reheat gently before serving.

makes 1½ cups (12 fl oz/375 ml)

butterscotch sauce

1 tablespoon (½ oz/20 g) sweet (unsalted) butter

2 fl oz (60 ml) light cornsyrup or golden syrup

2 tablespoons water

2 tablespoons packed brown sugar

❖ Place all the ingredients in a saucepan and stir over medium heat until the mixture is combined. Bring to a boil and boil, without stirring, for 3–4 minutes. Allow to cool slightly, then serve immediately.

makes 1 cup (8 fl oz/250 ml)

ginger brownies

makes 20

These unusual brownies
combine chewy dried fruits
with the crunch of cookie
pieces and nuts.

3 tablespoons (1½ oz/45 g) sweet (unsalted) butter

4 oz (125 g) semisweet (plain) chocolate, chopped

2 eggs

¾ cup (6 oz/185 g) granulated (white) sugar

1 teaspoon vanilla extract (essence)

¾ cup (3 oz/90 g) all-purpose (plain) flour, sifted

½ teaspoon baking powder

½ cup (2 oz/60 g) finely chopped walnuts

⅓ cup (2½ oz/75 g) chopped dried or
candied (glacé) figs

3 tablespoons (1½ oz/45 g) candied (glacé) ginger

12 chocolate fudge cookies, broken into pieces

❖ Preheat an oven to 350°F (180°C/Gas Mark 4). Butter an 8-inch (20-cm) square cake pan and line the base and sides with parchment (baking) paper.

❖ Heat the butter over a low heat until half melted, then stir in the chocolate until melted and combined. Remove from the heat and set aside.

❖ Beat the eggs until light and fluffy. Gradually add the sugar and beat until pale and thick, 3–4 minutes. Combine the melted chocolate and butter with the flour, baking powder, nuts, figs, ginger, and cookie pieces and fold into the egg mixture. Pour into the prepared pan. Bake for 40 minutes, or until the center of the top of the cake feels firm to the touch. Cool completely in the pan before turning out and cutting into small squares.

perfect partner

This easy-to-make sauce is delicious hot or cold. Serve it warm with ginger brownies (opposite) for dessert.

microwave pear and ginger sauce

6 pears, peeled, halved, and cored

1/4 cup (1 1/2 oz/45 g) firmly packed brown sugar

1–2 tablespoons finely chopped candied (glacé) ginger

1 tablespoon brandy

1 tablespoon chopped toasted almonds

❖ Place the pears, sugar, and ginger in a microwave-safe dish. Cover with a tight-fitting lid or plastic wrap and cook on high (100%) for 8–10 minutes, stirring several times during cooking. Allow to stand for 2 minutes. Using a fork, mash well, then stir in the brandy and toasted almonds.

makes about 2 1/2 cups (12 fl oz/750 ml)

chocolate brownies

with ice cream and chocolate sauce

serves 4

Vanilla ice cream sandwiched between rich, nut-studded brownies makes a delectable dessert. A drizzle of creamy chocolate sauce provides the finishing touch.

1 cup (8 oz/250 g) sweet (unsalted) butter

1¾ cups (14 oz/440 g) superfine (caster) sugar

4 eggs, lightly beaten

½ cup (1½ oz/45 g) unsweetened cocoa powder

2 cups (8 oz/250 g) all-purpose (plain) flour, sifted

2 teaspoons vanilla extract (essence)

13 oz (410 g) semisweet (plain) chocolate, chopped into small pieces

½ cup (2 oz/60 g) toasted hazelnuts

4 cups (32 fl oz/1 liter) vanilla ice cream

❖ Preheat an oven to 350°F (180°C/Gas Mark 4). Lightly butter a 9-inch (23-cm) square cake pan.

❖ For the brownies, melt the butter in a saucepan over low heat. Remove from the heat and stir in the sugar, eggs, cocoa powder, flour, and vanilla. Add the chopped chocolate and hazelnuts. Pour into the prepared pan and bake for 40–45 minutes, until a toothpick inserted in the center comes out clean. Allow to cool completely in pan. When cool, remove the brownies from the pan and cut into 8 rectangles.

❖ To serve, slice the ice cream into 4 rectangles, each the same size as a brownie. Place between 2 brownies and serve immediately with Chocolate Sauce (recipe at right) drizzled on top.

chocolate sauce

Once you've tried this sauce with the chocolate brownies (opposite), you'll find an endless list of other uses. Make double the recipe and store it in the refrigerator. Reheat gently before serving.

1/2 cup (4 fl oz/125 ml) heavy (double) cream

6 1/2 oz (185 g) semisweet (plain) chocolate, chopped into small pieces

❖ Heat the cream until just about to boil. Remove from the heat and add the chocolate. Let stand for 10 minutes, then stir until smooth.

mocha brownies

makes about 12

These quick-to-prepare brownies are an easy dessert to whip up when unexpected guests arrive.

BROWNIES

1 cup (8 oz/250 g) superfine (caster) sugar

1/2 cup (4 oz/125 g) butter

1/2 cup (2 oz/60 g) unsweetened cocoa powder

1 teaspoon instant coffee granules

2 eggs

1 teaspoon vanilla extract (essence)

1 1/2 cups (6 oz/185 g) all-purpose (plain) flour

1/2 teaspoon baking powder

1/4 teaspoon salt

1/2 cup (2 oz/60 g) chopped walnuts

FROSTING

3 tablespoons butter or margarine, softened

1/4 cup (3/4 oz/20 g) unsweetened cocoa powder

2 cups (8 oz/250 g) sifted confectioners' (icing) sugar

2–3 tablespoons milk

1/2 teaspoon vanilla extract (essence)

❖ Preheat an oven to 350°F (180°C/Gas Mark 4). Butter a 9 x 9 x 2-inch (23 x 23 x 5-cm) cake pan and line the base and sides with parchment (baking) paper.

❖ For brownies, In a medium saucepan combine the superfine sugar, butter, cocoa powder, and coffee granules. Cook and stir over medium heat until the butter melts. Remove from the heat; cool for 5 minutes. Add the eggs and vanilla. Using a wooden spoon, beat lightly by hand just until combined. Stir in the flour, baking powder, and salt. Stir in the walnuts. Spread the batter into the prepared pan. Bake for 25 minutes, or until set. Cool in the pan on a wire rack.

❖ For frosting, in a mixing bowl beat the butter or margarine until fluffy. Add the cocoa powder. Gradually add 1 cup (4 oz/125 g) of the confectioners' sugar, beating well. Slowly beat in 2 tablespoons of the milk and the vanilla. Slowly beat in the remaining sugar. Beat in additional milk, if necessary, to make a frosting of spreading consistency. Spread frosting over cooled brownies. Cut into bars.

recipe variation

Substitute the following icing for the frosting used with the mocha brownies (opposite).

coffee cream icing

2/3 cup (5 fl oz/155 ml) heavy (double) cream

1 tablespoon strong black coffee

1–2 tablespoons confectioners' (icing) sugar, sifted

❖ Whip the cream until soft peaks form. Fold in the coffee and then the sugar and mix well.

❖ Using a palette knife or a spatula, spread the icing evenly over the top of the cooled brownies.

flavored

These delectable flavored creams make an indulgent accompaniment for brownies. Add some fresh fruit for a simple but luscious dessert.

chocolate hazelnut cream

1¼ cups (10 fl oz/315 ml) heavy (double) cream, whipped

1 cup (125 g/4 oz) ground hazelnuts

4 oz (125 g) semisweet (plain) chocolate, melted and cooled

❖ Fold together the whipped cream, ground hazelnuts, and melted chocolate. Use immediately or cover and refrigerate for up to 2 days.

makes about 2½ cups (20 fl oz/625 ml)

berry cream

2½ cups (20 fl oz/600 ml) heavy (double) cream

½ lb (250 g) berries of your choice, in any combination

4 tablespoons superfine (caster) sugar

❖ In a bowl, whip the cream to soft peaks. Place the berries and sugar in the bowl of a food processor or blender and process to a purée. Strain the purée through a fine sieve into the cream. Beat the cream mixture until stiff. Use immediately or cover and refrigerate for up to 2 days.

makes about 3½ cups (28 fl oz/875 ml)

creams

almond cream

1/2 cup (3 oz/90 g) blanched almonds, toasted and cooled

3 tablespoons superfine (caster) sugar

2 tablespoons brandy

1 cup (8 fl oz/250 ml) heavy (double) cream, whipped

❖ In a food processor, process the almonds to a fine meal. Combine the sugar and brandy in a bowl and whisk until the sugar is dissolved. Fold in the cream, then the almonds. Use immediately or cover and refrigerate for up to 2 days.

makes 2 cups (16 fl oz/500 ml)

spiced whipped cream

1 cup (8 fl oz/250 ml) heavy (double) cream

1/2 teaspoon ground cinnamon, ground allspice, ground cardamom, or grated nutmeg, or to taste

❖ Whip the cream until soft peaks form. Stir in the preferred spice. Use immediately or cover and refrigerate for up to 2 days.

makes 1 1/2 cups (12 fl oz/375 ml)

vanilla cream

1 cup (8 fl oz/250 ml) heavy (double) cream, whipped

1 teaspoon vanilla extract (essence)

2 tablespoons confectioners' (icing) sugar, sifted

❖ Combine cream, vanilla, and sugar in a bowl and mix well. Use immediately or cover and refrigerate for up to 2 days.

makes about 1 1/2 cups (12 fl oz/375 ml)

ice cream
sandwiches

makes about 12

The ice cream will be much easier to work with if you let it soften slightly before packing it into the measuring cup. Let your imagination have free rein when choosing your ice cream flavor.

1 cup (8 oz/250 g) butter or margarine, softened

2/3 cup (5 oz/155 g) superfine (caster) sugar

1 egg

1/4 cup (3 oz/90 g) honey

1 1/2 cups (6 oz/185 g) all-purpose (plain) flour

2 teaspoons baking powder

1/4 teaspoon salt

3/4 cup (2 1/2 oz/75 g) rolled oats

1/2 cup (3 oz/90 g) semisweet (plain) chocolate chips and/or raisins and/or chopped dried fruit

1 qt (1 liter) vanilla, chocolate, rum raisin, chocolate chip, or your choice of ice cream, softened

❖ Preheat an oven to 375°F (190°C/Gas Mark 4).

❖ In a mixing bowl beat the butter or margarine with an electric mixer on medium to high speed for 30 seconds. Add the sugar; beat until combined. Beat in the egg and honey. Sift together the flour, baking powder and salt and add to the butter mixture, beating in as much of the flour as you can with the mixer. Stir in any remaining flour with a wooden spoon. Stir in the oats and chocolate and/or raisins and/or dried fruit.

❖ Drop rounded tablespoons of the dough 3 inches (7.5 cm) apart on ungreased baking sheets. Bake for 12–15 minutes, or until golden brown. Cool on baking sheets for 1 minute then remove with a spatula and transfer to wire racks to cool completely.

❖ To make each cookie sandwich, pack softened ice cream into a ⅓-cup (3-fl oz/80-ml) measure or small ramekin and unmold it onto the flat side of a cookie. Top with a second cookie, flat-side down. Press cookies together. Wrap each sandwich in plastic wrap; freeze for about 1 hour, or until the ice cream is solid, then serve.

chocolate butter spritz

makes about 60

Pressed, or "spritz," cookies, are an old Scandinavian specialty, but have become a favorite in many other countries, too. These buttery cookies with their dainty, fanciful shapes are hard to resist—it's just as well the recipe makes so many. For more information on pressed cookies, see pages 298–299.

1 cup (8 oz/250 g) butter or margarine, softened

1/2 cup (2 oz/60 g) sifted confectioners' (icing) sugar

1/2 cup (3½ oz/105 g) packed brown sugar

1/4 cup (1 oz/30 g) unsweetened cocoa powder

1 egg yolk

2 tablespoons crème de cacao or milk

1 teaspoon vanilla extract (essence)

2¼ cups (10 oz/315 g) all-purpose (plain) flour

chocolate sprinkles or finely chopped nuts (optional)

❖ Preheat an oven to 375°F (190°C/Gas Mark 4).

❖ In a large mixing bowl beat the butter or margarine with an electric mixer on medium to high speed for 30 seconds. Add the confectioners' sugar, brown sugar, and cocoa powder; beat until combined. Beat in the egg yolk, crème de cacao or milk, and vanilla. Beat in as much of the flour as you can with the mixer. Stir in any remaining flour with a wooden spoon.

❖ Pack the dough into a cookie press fitted with the desired plate. Force the dough through the press onto ungreased baking sheets, spacing the cookies 1 inch (2.5 cm) apart. Change the plate partway through if you want more than one shape. (It is easier and less messy to do this after the press is emptied of one batch of dough; change the plate, refill the press, then proceed). If desired, sprinkle with chocolate sprinkles or chopped nuts.

❖ Bake for 8–10 minutes, or until the edges of cookies are firm but not brown. Transfer to a wire rack to cool.

recipe hints

Dough for spritz cookies should always be at room temperature, as chilled dough is too stiff to push through the press easily.

If you're in a hurry, you can also make these as drop cookies simply by dropping rounded teaspoonfuls of the dough onto the baking sheets.

white chocolate apricot rugelach

makes about 36

These pastry-like goodies are a treat for breakfast or with morning coffee as well as after dinner. Choose your favorite flavor of jam or marmalade for the filling, or make part of the mixture with one flavor and the rest with another.

2 cups (8 oz/250 g) all-purpose (plain) flour

¾ cup (6 oz/185 g) cold butter or margarine, chopped

½ cup (4 fl oz/125 ml) sour cream

1 teaspoon vanilla extract (essence)

⅓ cup (3½ oz/105 g) apricot or raspberry jam
or orange marmalade

½ cup (3 oz/90 g) white chocolate, finely chopped

2 tablespoons granulated (white) sugar

1 teaspoon ground cinnamon (optional)

❖ Preheat an oven to 375°F (190°C/Gas Mark 4).

❖ Sift the flour into a mixing bowl. With a pastry blender or 2 knives, cut in the butter or margarine until the mixture resembles small peas. Stir in the sour cream and vanilla just until the dough holds together. Turn the dough out onto a lightly floured surface and knead gently about 10 times.

❖ Divide the dough into thirds. Wrap two of the portions in plastic wrap and set aside while you roll out the third portion on a lightly floured surface into a 10-inch (25-cm) circle. Spread the dough with a scant 2 tablespoons of the jam or marmalade. Sprinkle with one-third of the chopped white chocolate. Cut the dough into 12 wedges. Starting at the curved edge, roll up each wedge. Place, point-side down, 2 inches (5 cm) apart on an ungreased baking sheet. Repeat with the remaining dough, jam or marmalade, and white chocolate.

❖ In a small mixing bowl stir together the sugar and, if desired, cinnamon; sprinkle a little of the mixture over each cookie.

❖ Bake for 20–25 minutes, or until light golden brown. Remove the cookies from the baking sheets and transfer to a wire rack to cool. Store in an airtight container.

mocha tea cookies

makes about 36

The word "mocha", which denotes a chocolate–coffee combination, comes from the name of a port in Yemen where coffee trees were first cultivated. In this easy recipe, cocoa powder provides the chocolate flavor and instant espresso powder the coffee.

¾ cup (6 oz/185 g) butter or margarine, softened

⅓ cup (2½ oz/75 g) packed brown sugar

⅓ cup (1 oz/30 g) unsweetened cocoa powder

1 teaspoon instant espresso coffee powder

1 teaspoon vanilla extract (essence)

⅛ teaspoon salt

1¾ cups (7 oz/220 g) all-purpose (plain) flour

ICING

3 tablespoons butter or margarine

2¼ cups (9 oz/280 g) sifted confectioners' (icing) sugar

1 teaspoon vanilla extract (essence)

1–2 tablespoons milk

❖ Preheat an oven to 375°F (190°C/Gas Mark 4). Lightly butter 2 baking sheets or line them with parchment (baking) paper.

❖ For the cookies, in a large mixing bowl beat the butter with an electric mixer on medium to high speed for 30 seconds. Add the brown sugar, cocoa powder, espresso powder, vanilla, and salt; beat until combined. Beat in as much of the flour as you can with the mixer. Stir in any remaining flour with a wooden spoon. Shape the dough into a 10-inch (25-cm) roll. Wrap in waxed paper or plastic wrap. Chill for 2 hours, or until firm.

❖ Cut the log into ¼-inch (6-mm) thick slices. Place slices about 2 inches (5 cm) apart on the prepared baking sheets. Bake for 8–10 minutes, or until the edges are firm and the bottoms are lightly browned. Remove the cookies from the trays and transfer to a wire rack to cool.

❖ For the icing, in a saucepan melt the butter and stir over medium heat until it browns. Remove from the heat; stir in the confectioners' sugar, vanilla, and enough of the milk to give a spreading consistency. If the icing becomes too stiff, add hot water, a few drops at a time, and stir until smooth. Using a palette knife, top each cooled cookie with some of the icing, smoothing the icing, or swirling the knife to create a textured surface if preferred. Store in an airtight container.

afghans

makes about 25

These cookies combine chocolate, coconut, and cornflakes. They can be spooned onto the baking trays for a rustic, knobbly effect, or rolled into balls for a smoother cookie. The recipe can easily be doubled.

1/2 cup (4 oz/125 g) butter

1/3 cup (2 1/2 oz/75 g) superfine (caster) sugar

1 teaspoon vanilla extract (essence)

1 egg

1/2 cup (2 oz/60 g) self-rising flour

1/2 cup (2 oz/60 g) all-purpose (plain) flour

2 tablespoons unsweetened cocoa powder

1 1/2 cups (2 oz/60 g) cornflakes, lightly crushed

1/4 cup (1 oz/30 g) grated dried (desiccated) coconut

CHOCOLATE ICING

5 oz (155 g) semisweet (plain) chocolate chips

1 tablespoon (20 g) butter or solid vegetable shortening

25 walnut halves

❖ Preheat an oven to 360°F (180°C/Gas Mark 4). Lightly butter 2 baking sheets or line them with parchment (baking) paper.

❖ Cream the butter, sugar, and vanilla until light and creamy. Lightly beat in the egg, a little at a time, until thoroughly incorporated.

❖ Sift together the flours and cocoa powder. Fold into the butter mixture. Stir in the cornflakes and coconut. Drop level tablespoons of the mixture on the prepared baking sheets, or roll level tablespoons into balls and place on the baking sheets, spacing them about 1 inch (2.5 cm) apart.

❖ Bake for 15 minutes, or until the cookies are a little darker in color and firm to the touch. Using a spatula, transfer to a wire rack to cool completely.

❖ Meanwhile, for the icing, melt the chocolate chips and butter or vegetable shortening in a heatproof bowl over simmering water. Mix to combine. Using the back of a spoon, swirl the icing over the cooled cookies and top each with a walnut half.

chocolate peanut cookies

makes about 20

To remove the skins from the peanuts for this recipe, place the nuts in a clean kitchen towel, gather up the corners of the towel to enclose the nuts, then rub vigorously to remove the skins. Don't worry if not all of the skins come off. Alternatively, the peanuts may be left with their skins on if you prefer.

1/2 cup (4 oz/125 g) butter, softened

1 cup (8 oz/250 g) superfine (caster) sugar

1 teaspoon vanilla extract (essence)

1 egg, lightly beaten

1 1/2 cups (6 oz/185g) all-purpose (plain) flour

1 teaspoon baking powder

2 tablespoons unsweetened cocoa powder

1 cup (5 oz/155 g) raw peanuts, skinned and roughly chopped

CHOCOLATE GLACÉ ICING

1 cup (4 oz/125 g) confectioners' (icing) sugar

1 tablespoon unsweetened cocoa powder

1 tablespoon (20 g) butter, melted

1/2 cup (2 oz/60 g) grated dried (desiccated) coconut, lightly toasted

✣ Preheat oven to 250°F (180°C/Gas Mark 4). Line a large baking tray with parchment (baking) paper or greaseproof paper.

✣ Using an electric mixer, cream the butter, sugar, and vanilla on medium to high speed until lIght and creamy. Add the egg a little at a time, beating well after each addition.

✣ Fold in the combined and sifted flour, baking powder, and cocoa. Stir in the peanuts. Place level tablespoons of the mixture on the prepared baking sheet, spacing them about 2 inches (5 cm) apart.

✣ Bake for about 15 minutes, or until golden brown. Leave to cool on the baking sheet for 5 minutes, then transfer to a wire rack to cool completely.

✣ For the icing, combine the sifted confectioners' sugar and cocoa in a small bowl. Add the butter and a little hot water if necessary to give a spreadable consistency.

✣ Using the back of a teaspoon, swirl the icing over each cooled cookie. Top with a little of the grated coconut. Place the iced cookies back on the wire rack until the icing is set. Store in an airtight container.

butter, spice, *and* honey cookies

sugar cookies

makes about 40

2 1/2 cups (9 oz/280 g)
all-purpose (plain) flour

2/3 cup (5 1/2 oz/170 g) cold
sweet (unsalted) butter,
chopped

pinch salt

3 tablespoons superfine
(caster) sugar

2 egg yolks beaten with
4 tablespoons (2 fl oz/
60 ml) ice-cold water

confectioners' (icing)
sugar (optional)

❖ Preheat an oven to 400°F (200°C/Gas Mark 6). Line baking sheets with parchment (baking) paper.

❖ In the bowl of a food processor, process the flour and butter until coarse crumbs form. Add the salt and sugar and process again until just combined; do not overprocess the mixture. With the motor running, add the egg yolk mixture and process using the pulse button until a ball of pastry forms. Turn out onto a work surface, wrap in plastic wrap, and chill for 30 minutes.

❖ Roll the pastry out to a 1/4-inch (6-mm) thickness. With a 2-inch (5-cm) cookie cutter or a sharp knife, cut into desired shapes. Place on the prepared baking sheets. Bake for 10–15 minutes or until golden. Let the cookies rest on the baking tray for 2–3 minutes, then transfer to wire racks to cool completely. When cool, store in an airtight container. Serve with coffee or ice cream. If desired, sprinkle with confectioners' (icing) sugar just before serving.

cinnamon
crisps

makes about 36

**These delicate little cookies
are simplicity itself, and can
be varied according to your
whim (see sidebar, page 79).
The only trick is to check
them frequently toward the
end of the cooking time, as
they burn easily.**

²/₃ cup (5 oz/155 g) butter, softened

¹/₃ cup (3 oz/90 g) superfine (caster) sugar

1½ cups (6 oz/185 g) self-rising flour

½ cup (2 oz/60 g) ground almonds

1 teaspoon ground cinnamon

pinch salt

❖ Preheat an oven to 350°F (180°C/Gas Mark 4). Lightly butter baking sheets or line them with parchment (baking) paper.

❖ Using an electric mixer on medium speed, cream the butter and sugar until just combined. Sift together the flour, ground almonds, cinnamon, and salt and add to the butter-and-sugar mixture. Using a wooden spoon, mix well.

❖ Turn out onto a lightly floured work surface and roll out between 2 sheets of parchment (baking) paper to a thickness of ⅛ inch (3 mm). Or, form the mixture into a log, wrap in plastic wrap, and chill for 30 minutes before cutting into slices ⅛ inch (3 mm) thick.

❖ Place the cookies on the prepared baking sheets and bake until lightly golden, 12–15 minutes. Check them frequently, as they burn easily. Let them cool on the trays for 5 minutes, then transfer to a wire rack to cool completely.

recipe variation

Replace the ground cinnamon with any of the following:
- 1 teaspoon grated orange rind or 1 teaspoon orange flower water
- 1 teaspoon grated lemon and/or lime rind
- 1 teaspoon almond extract (essence)

gingerbread
biscuits

makes 30–40

These rich and spicy cookies
are favorites with children
and adults alike. The firm
dough lends itself well to
rolling and cutting and can
be cut into plain rounds or
fanciful shapes adorned with
colored icing, sprinkles,
currants, chocolate chips, or
pieces of dried fruit.

1/2 cup (6 oz/185 g) light molasses (treacle) or honey

1/2 cup (3 1/2 oz/105 g) firmly packed brown sugar

2 tablespoons (1 oz/30 g) sweet (unsalted) butter

2 1/2 cups (12 oz/375 g) all-purpose (plain) flour

2 teaspoons ground ginger

pinch ground cinnamon

pinch ground cloves

pinch ground cardamom

1 egg yolk

1 teaspoon baking soda (bicarbonate of soda)

1 tablespoon tepid water

❖ Preheat an oven to 325°F (160°C/Gas Mark 3). Lightly butter baking trays.

❖ In a saucepan over low heat, combine the molasses, treacle, or honey, sugar, and butter and stir gently until the butter is melted and the sugar dissolved. Allow to cool.

❖ Sift together two-thirds of the flour, the ginger, cinnamon, cloves, and cardamom into a mixing bowl. Add the egg yolk and honey mixture and stir to combine.

❖ Dissolve the baking soda in the water and add to the flour mixture. Slowly knead in as much of the remaining flour as needed to obtain a firm dough. Turn out onto a lightly floured work surface and roll out to a thickness of ½ inch (12 mm). Cut out desired shapes. Place on the prepared baking sheets and bake for 10–12 minutes. Allow to cool on the baking sheets for 5 minutes, then transfer to a wire rack to cool completely.

❖ If desired, ice and decorate cooled cookies. Store in an airtight container.

pecan shortbread

makes 8

This buttery biscuit cake is of Scottish origin. Its name is derived from its crumbly texture, which is achieved by minimal handling during the mixing of the ingredients, thereby "shortening" the development of toughening proteins in the flour. Traditionally, shortbread contains only butter, sugar, and flour, but pecans are a delicious addition.

1 cup (8 oz/250 g) butter, softened

2/3 cup (5 oz/155 g) confectioners' (icing) sugar

2 cups (8 oz/250 g) all-purpose (plain) flour

1/2 cup (2 oz/60 g) roughly chopped pecans

❖ Preheat an oven to 325°F (160°C/Gas Mark 3). Lightly butter a baking sheet.

❖ Using electric beaters on medium to high speed, cream the butter and sugar until light and creamy, 2–3 minutes. Use a large metal spoon to fold in the flour in 3–4 batches. Using a wooden spoon, mix to a soft dough, incorporating the pecans.

❖ Turn the dough out onto a floured work surface and knead lightly and briefly until smooth. Flatten with floured hands into a 6-inch (15-cm) circle and place on the prepared baking sheet.

❖ Using a rolling pin, roll the dough out further into a neat 7-inch (18-cm) circle. With a sharp knife, mark the surface of the shortbread into 8 even wedges. Prick the shortbread evenly all over with a fork.

❖ Bake until pale and firm, 30–35 minutes. While still warm, cut the wedges along the score marks all the way through. Let cool completely on the baking sheet.

coconut shortbread

makes 8

The recipe given here elaborates upon shortbread's traditional simplicity with the addition of coconut for a subtle flavor accent.

1 cup (4 oz/125 g) all-purpose (plain) flour

¼ cup (1½ oz/45 g) rice flour

⅛ teaspoon salt

⅓ cup (3 oz/90 g) granulated (white) sugar

¼ cup (1 oz/30 g) unsweetened grated dried (desiccated) coconut

½ cup (4 oz/125 g) chilled sweet (unsalted) butter, cut into pieces

½ teaspoon vanilla extract (essence)

½ teaspoon almond extract (essence)

❖ Preheat an oven to 350°F (180°C/Gas Mark 4). Lightly butter a baking sheet.

❖ Sift together the flours, salt, and sugar into a bowl, then sift together again into another bowl. Add the coconut and butter and, using a pastry blender or 2 forks, cut them in until the mixture is crumbly. Add the vanilla and almond extracts and knead the mixture in the bowl to form a tender dough mass. Do not overmix or the dough will toughen.

❖ Place the dough on the prepared baking sheet and shape it into a round 7–8 inches (18–20 cm) in diameter and about ½ inch (12 mm) thick. Using your fingers, pinch around the edges to create an attractive border. With a sharp, long-bladed knife, score the round into 8 equal wedges. Prick the surface lightly all over with a fork.

❖ Bake until a nice pale gold and slightly firm to the touch, 20–25 minutes. Remove from the oven and, while still warm, cut along the score marks. Serve warm or at room temperature.

chinese almond cookies

makes 24

Almonds have been cultivated in China for at least 1500 years. As well as being used in savory dishes, they are often ground and combined with milk in desserts. The technique of baking, as in this recipe, is borrowed from the West.

¾ cup (6 oz/185 g) butter or margarine, softened

¼ cup (2 oz/60 g) superfine (caster) sugar

½ cup (3½ oz/105 g) lightly packed brown sugar

1 egg yolk

½ teaspoon almond extract (essence)

2 cups (8 oz/250 g) all-purpose (plain) flour

½ teaspoon baking powder

sesame seeds

24 blanched almond halves

❖ Preheat an oven to 350°F (180°C/Gas Mark 4). Lightly butter a baking sheet, or line it with parchment (baking) paper.

❖ In a medium bowl, cream the butter or margarine, superfine sugar, and brown sugar. Add the egg yolk and almond extract and beat until fluffy.

❖ Sift the flour and baking powder together. Using a wooden spoon, fold the flour into the butter mixture a little at a time. When all the flour is incorporated, beat lightly to make a smooth dough. Do not work the mixture too much, or the cookies will be tough.

❖ Divide the dough equally into 24 portions, then, with hands dampened with a little water, shape each portion into a walnut-sized ball. Dip the tops of the cookies in the sesame seeds. (You may need to slightly dampen the top of each with a little water.) Lightly press half an almond into the center of each cookie and flatten the cookie a little.

❖ Place the cookies about 1 inch (2.5 cm) apart on the prepared baking sheet. Bake for 8–10 minutes or until golden brown. Store in airtight containers.

koulourakia

makes about 48

When visiting a Greek home, you might be welcomed with this licorice-flavored cookie along with a small cup of strong coffee and a glass of cold water.

¾ cup (6 oz/185 g) butter or margarine, softened

¾ cup (6 oz/185 g) granulated (white) sugar

2 teaspoons baking powder

1 teaspoon aniseed liqueur such as Ouzo

1 teaspoon finely shredded lemon zest (rind)

2 eggs

2 tablespoons milk

3 cups (12 oz/375 g) all-purpose (plain) flour

1 lightly beaten egg white

1 tablespoon milk

3 tablespoons sesame seeds (optional)

❖ Preheat an oven to 375°F (190°C/Gas Mark 4). Lightly butter baking sheets or line them with parchment (baking) paper.

❖ In a large mixing bowl beat the butter or margarine with an electric mixer on medium to high speed for 30 seconds. Add the sugar, baking powder, aniseed liqueur, and lemon zest; beat until combined. Beat in the eggs and the 2 tablespoons milk. Beat in as much of the flour as you can with the mixer. Stir in any remaining flour with a wooden spoon. Divide the dough in half. If necessary, chill it for 30–60 minutes, or until firm and easy to handle.

❖ On a lightly floured surface, shape each half of dough into a 12-inch (30-cm) log. Cut each log into twenty-four ½-inch (12-mm) pieces. Roll each piece into a 6-inch (15-cm) rope. Curl each end of the rope to form an S shape. Place the cookies 1 inch (2.5 cm) apart on the prepared baking sheets.

❖ In a small mixing bowl stir together the egg white and 1 tablespoon milk; brush the mixture over the cookies. If desired, sprinkle cookies with sesame seeds.

❖ Bake for 7–9 minutes, or until bottoms are lightly browned. Remove cookies from the baking sheets and transfer to a wire rack to cool completely.

melting moments

makes 30 double cookies

True to their name, these easy-to-make buttery delights take only moments to melt in the mouth. Use only butter, not margarine, to produce the finest results.

1 cup (8 oz/250 g) butter

1/2 cup (2 oz/60 g) confectioners' (icing) sugar

1/2 cup (2 oz/60 g) cornstarch (cornflour)

1 1/2 cups (6 oz/185 g) all-purpose (plain) flour

CHOCOLATE CREAM FROSTING

2 oz (60 g) bittersweet or semisweet (plain) chocolate

1/4 cup (2 oz/60 g) butter

1 cup (4 oz/125 g) confectioners' (icing) sugar

❖ Preheat an oven to 350°F (180°C/Gas Mark 4). Lightly butter baking sheets.

❖ Using an electric mixer on medium to high speed, cream the butter and sugar until the mixture is light and fluffy. Sift the cornstarch and flour together over the butter mixture and stir in lightly with a metal spoon. Transfer to a piping bag fitted with a star tube. Pipe the dough in rosettes onto the prepared tray. Bake for about 12 minutes until pale golden and dry to the touch. Remove from the baking sheets and transfer to a wire rack to cool. When completely cool, sandwich together with the frosting. Store in an airtight container for up to 1 week.

❖ To make the frosting, melt the chocolate over a double boiler or in a microwave oven. Add the butter and sugar and, using a wooden spoon, beat to a smooth cream. Spread the flat side of half the cookies with the cream, pressing unfrosted ones on top.

recipe variation

Roll the dough into walnut-sized balls and place on prepared baking sheets, spacing the cookies about 2 inches (5 cm) apart. Top each cookie with half a maraschino (glacé) cherry, half a blanched almond, or a hazelnut. Bake as directed (see left). Remove from the baking sheets and transfer to a wire rack to cool. Omit the chocolate frosting.

Makes about 60 single cookies

holiday cookies

makes 36–48

Children will have a great time helping decorate the myriad shapes that can be cut from this basic cookie dough. For festive occasions, use appropriately shaped cutters, and let whimsy rule when you ice the cookies.

¾ cup (6 oz/185 g) butter or margarine, softened

¾ cup (6 oz/185 g) superfine (caster) sugar

1 teaspoon baking powder

¼ teaspoon salt

1 egg

1 tablespoon milk

1 teaspoon vanilla extract (essence)

2 cups (8 oz/250 g) all-purpose (plain) flour

ICING

1 cup (4 oz/125 g) sifted confectioners' (icing) sugar

¼ teaspoon vanilla extract (essence)

1 tablespoon milk

few drops food coloring, in various colors (optional)

❖ Preheat an oven to 375°F (190°C/Gas Mark 4).

❖ For the cookies, in a large mixing bowl beat the butter or margarine with an electric mixer on medium to high speed for 30 seconds. Add the sugar, baking powder, and salt; beat until combined. Beat in the egg, milk, and vanilla. Beat in as much of the flour as you can with the mixer. Stir in any remaining flour with a wooden spoon. Divide the dough in half. Cover with plastic wrap and chill for 3 hours, or until the dough is easy to handle.

❖ On a lightly floured surface, roll out one half of the dough to an ⅛-inch (3-mm) thickness. Using 2- or 2½-inch (5- or 6-cm) cutters, cut the dough into desired holiday shapes, such as hearts, shamrocks, eggs, rabbits, flags, angels, or stars. Place cookies 1 inch (2.5 cm) apart on ungreased baking sheets. Repeat with the remaining portion of dough.

❖ Bake for 7–8 minutes, or until edges are firm and bottoms are lightly browned. Remove cookies from the baking sheets and transfer to a wire rack to cool.

❖ Meanwhile, for the icing, in a small bowl stir together the confectioners' sugar, vanilla, and enough of the milk to make an icing of piping consistency. If desired, color the icing: Divide it into batches, one for each color that you are using, and place each batch into a separate small bowl. Add the food coloring and stir until the color is evenly distributed and no streaks remain. Use a piping bag and writing nozzle to decorate cookies with icing.

honey
snowflakes

makes about 50

**For this unusual recipe, the
"frosting" cooks together
with the cookie. Don't
worry about making too
many; they keep very well.**

½ cup (4 oz/125 g) butter or margarine, softened

½ cup (3½ oz/105 g) lightly packed brown sugar

1 teaspoon baking powder

½ teaspoon ground cardamom

1 egg, lightly beaten

½ cup (6 fl oz/185 ml) honey

2 cups (8 oz/250 g) all-purpose (plain) flour

1 cup (4 oz/125 g) whole-grain (wholemeal) flour

FROSTING

¼ cup (2 oz/60 g) butter or margarine, softened

¼ cup (1 oz/30 g) all-purpose (plain) flour

2 teaspoons water

❖ Preheat an oven to 375°F (190°C/Gas Mark 4).

❖ For cookies, in a mixing bowl beat the butter or margarine with an electric mixer on medium to high speed for 30 seconds. Add the brown sugar, baking powder, and cardamom; beat until combined. Beat in the egg and honey. Beat in as much of the combined flours as you can with a mixer. Stir in any remaining flour with a wooden spoon. Divide dough in half. Cover and chill for 3 hours, or until easy to handle.

❖ For frosting, in a mixing bowl stir together the butter or margarine, flour, and water to make a smooth batter.

❖ On a lightly floured surface, roll each half of dough to a ¼-inch (6-mm) thickness. Using a 2- or 2½-inch (5- or 6-cm) 6-pointed star or scalloped round cutter, cut dough into shapes. Place cookies 2 inches (5 cm) apart on ungreased baking sheets. Using a piping bag and writing nozzle, pipe frosting on unbaked cookies.

❖ Bake for 7–9 minutes, or until edges are firm and bottoms are lightly browned. Using a spatula, transfer to a wire rack to cool.

spice cookies

makes about 48

These rich cookies, flavored
with lemon and spices, make
a tasty treat for afternoon
tea or the kids' lunchboxes.
The recipe makes plenty,
and they keep well.

1/2 cup (4 oz/125 g) butter

3/4 cup (6 oz/185 g) superfine (caster) sugar

1 egg

1/2 teaspoon lemon extract (essence)

1/2 cup (4 fl oz/125 ml) evaporated milk

1 tablespoon vinegar

2 1/2 cups (10 oz/315 g) all-purpose (plain) flour

1 teaspoon baking powder

1/2 teaspoon salt

1/4 teaspoon baking soda (bicarbonate of soda)

1/2 teaspoon nutmeg

1/2 teaspoon cinnamon

❖ Preheat an oven to 350°F (180°C/Gas Mark 4). Lightly butter 2 baking sheets or line them with parchment (baking) paper.

❖ Using an electric mixer on medium to high speed, cream the butter and sugar until light and fluffy. Beat in the egg and lemon extract.

❖ In a cup, combine the milk and vinegar.

❖ In a large bowl, sift together the flour, baking powder, salt, baking soda, nutmeg, and cinnamon.

❖ Using a wooden spoon, fold the sifted dry ingredients alternately with the milk-and-vinegar mixture into the butter-and sugar-mixture. Stir until just combined.

❖ Drop heaping teaspoons of the mixture onto the prepared baking sheets. Bake for 15–20 minutes or until lightly browned. Using a spatula, transfer to wire racks to cool.

aniseed
cookies

makes 8

These cookies, known in Spain as *tortas de anis*, are especially popular in Andalusia. They are made by the most highly regarded confectioners and are characterized by sulfurized paper wrappers. Although the commercially produced ones are delicious, these cookies are very quick and easy to make at home.

¼ cup (2 fl oz/60 ml) olive oil

¼ cup (2 fl oz/60 ml) beer

1 tablespoon dry anisette liqueur (similar to grappa)

1 teaspoon salt

1 cup (4 oz/125 g) all-purpose (plain) flour

½ cup (80 g) sesame seeds

½ cup (80 g) aniseeds

⅔ cup (5 oz/155 g) superfine (caster) sugar

❖ Preheat an oven to 400°F (200°C/Gas Mark 5). Preheat a broiler (grill). Lightly butter 2 baking sheets.

❖ In a large bowl, combine the oil, beer, anisette, and salt. Add the sifted flour gradually. Using your hands, mix to a dough. Turn out onto a work surface and knead briefly. Divide the dough into 8 pieces.

❖ Flour the work surface and roll out the pieces, one at a time, starting in the center and working outward, to form very thin rounds. Sprinkle on the sesame seeds, aniseeds, and sugar. Roll again to press the seeds firmly into the dough, then trim the edges neatly. Using a spatula, transfer the cookies to the prepared baking sheets. Bake for about 8 minutes, watching carefully in case they burn.

❖ When the cookies are almost ready, remove the baking sheet from the oven and put it under the broiler for 2 minutes to caramelize the sugar. Using a spatula, immediately transfer the cookies to a wire rack to cool.

makes about 48

½ cup (4 oz/125 g) butter or margarine, softened

¾ cup (6 oz/185 g) packed brown sugar

1 teaspoon ground cinnamon

¼ teaspoon baking powder

1 egg

1 teaspoon vanilla extract

2 cups (8 oz/250 g) all-purpose (plain) flour

1 tablespoon superfine (caster) sugar

½ teaspoon ground cinnamon

1 lightly beaten egg white

96 miniature chocolate chips or dried currants (optional)

❖ Preheat an oven to 375°F (190°C/Gas Mark 4).

❖ In a mixing bowl beat the butter or margarine with an electric mixer on medium to high speed for 30 seconds. Add the brown sugar, 1 teaspoon cinnamon, and baking powder; beat until combined. Beat in the egg and vanilla. Beat in as much of the flour as you can with the mixer. Stir in any remaining flour with a wooden spoon. Divide dough in half.

❖ On a lightly floured surface, shape each portion of dough into a 12-inch (30-cm) log. Cut each log into twenty-four ½-inch (12-mm) pieces. Roll each piece into a 6-inch (15-cm) rope. Coil each rope into a snail shape: With one end, make a small coil for the eye; coil the other end in the opposite direction to make the body. Place the cookies 2 inches (5 cm) apart on lightly greased baking sheets. Brush with egg white. In a small mixing bowl stir together the superfine sugar and ½ teaspoon cinnamon. Sprinkle over the cookies. If desired, decorate with 2 chocolate chips or currants to make the eyes.

❖ Bake for 8 minutes, or until edges of cookies are firm and bottoms are lightly browned. Cool on a wire rack.

cinnamon
snails

raspberry pinwheels

makes about 32

½ cup (4 oz/125 g) butter or margarine, softened

½ cup (4 oz/125 g) superfine (caster) sugar

1 teaspoon baking powder

1 egg

1 teaspoon vanilla extract (essence)

2 cups (8 oz/250 g) all-purpose (plain) flour

⅓ cup (3 fl oz/80 ml) seedless raspberry, strawberry, or apricot jam

¼ cup (1½ oz/45 g) finely chopped pistachio nuts or almonds

❖ Preheat an oven to 350°F (180°C/Gas Mark 4).

❖ In a mixing bowl beat the butter or margarine with an electric mixer on medium to high speed for 30 seconds. Add the sugar and baking powder; beat until combined. Beat in the egg and vanilla. Beat in as much of the flour as you can with the mixer. Stir in any remaining flour with a wooden spoon. Divide the dough in half. Cover and chill for about 3 hours, or until it is easy to handle.

❖ On a lightly floured surface, roll each half of the dough into a 10-inch (25-cm) square (using a sharp knife, trim to exact dimensions). Using a pastry wheel or sharp knife, cut each square into sixteen 2½-inch (6-cm) squares. Place ½ inch (12 mm) apart on ungreased baking sheets. Cut 1-inch (2.5-cm) slits from each corner to center. Drop ½ teaspoon of the jam in each center. Fold every other tip to the center to form a pinwheel. Sprinkle chopped nuts in the center and press firmly to seal.

❖ Bake for 8–10 minutes, or until the edges are firm and lightly browned. Cool on baking sheets for 1 minute. Remove cookies from the baking sheets and transfer to a wire rack to cool.

shortbread

makes 8

1 cup (8 oz/250 g) butter,
softened

⅔ cup (5 oz/155 g) superfine
(caster) sugar, plus 2 teaspoons
extra

2 cups (8 oz/250 g) all-purpose
(plain) flour

❖ Preheat an oven to 325°F (160°C/Gas Mark 3).
Lightly butter a baking sheet.

❖ Cream the butter and the ⅔ cup sugar with
an electric mixer on medium to high speed until
light and creamy, 2–3 minutes. Use a large metal
spoon to fold in the flour in 3–4 batches. Mix to
a soft dough.

LEFT: plain shortbread;
RIGHT: pecan shortbread (page 82)

❖ Turn the dough out onto a floured work surface and knead lightly and briefly until smooth. Flatten with floured hands into a 6-inch (15-cm) circle and place on the prepared baking sheet.

❖ Using a rolling pin, roll the dough out further into a neat 7-inch (18-cm) circle. With floured fingers, pinch the edges decoratively to form the traditional "petticoat" shape. Sprinkle with the extra 2 teaspoons superfine sugar. With a sharp knife, mark the surface of the shortbread into 8 even wedges.

❖ Bake until pale and firm, about 40 minutes. While still warm, cut the wedges along the score marks all the way through. Let cool completely on the baking sheet.

madeleines

makes about 36

²⁄₃ cup (5 oz/155 g) butter

2 eggs

²⁄₃ cup (5 oz/155 g) superfine (caster) sugar

finely grated zest (rind) of 1 lemon

1¼ cups (5 oz/155 g) all-purpose (plain) flour

½ teaspoon baking powder

Confectioners' (icing) sugar

❖ Preheat an oven to 450°F (220°C/Gas Mark 6). Lightly butter 36 madeleine molds, then dust them lightly with flour, shaking out any excess. Omit this step if using nonstick molds.

❖ Melt the butter and let it cool slightly. In a bowl, whisk the eggs, sugar, and lemon zest until thick and pale. Sift in half the combined sifted flour and baking powder. Fold in gently with a large metal spoon. Pour half the butter round the sides of the bowl and fold in. Repeat with the remaining flour and baking powder, then with the remaining butter. Do not overmix.

❖ Leave to stand for 5 minutes. Place spoonfuls in the molds, filling them to just level with the top. Bake until firm and golden, 8–10 minutes. Cool for 2–3 minutes in the molds, then carefully remove and transfer to a wire rack to cool completely.

❖ Just before serving, sift confectioners' sugar lightly over the tops of the madeleines.

LEFT: plain madeleines;
RIGHT: chocolate madeleines (page 124)

brandy snaps
with pastry cream

makes 20

2 tablespoons cornsyrup, light
molasses, or golden syrup

¼ cup (2 oz/60 g)
sweet (unsalted) butter

⅓ cup (2½ oz/75 g) packed
brown sugar

¼ cup (1 oz/30 g) all-purpose
(plain) flour, sifted

1½ teaspoons ground ginger

PASTRY CREAM

3 egg yolks

¼ cup (2 oz/60 g) sugar

2½ tablespoons all-purpose
(plain) flour

1 cup (8 fl oz/250 ml) milk

1 teaspoon vanilla extract
(essence)

❖ Preheat an oven to 350°F (180°C/Gas Mark 4). Lightly butter 2 baking sheets.

❖ Place the syrup, butter, and brown sugar into a saucepan and stir over low heat until the butter is melted. Remove from the heat and stir in the flour and ginger. For each snap, drop two teaspoons of mixture onto the prepared baking sheets, 3–4 inches (7–10 cm) apart. Make only 3–4 snaps at a time. Bake for 5 minutes then remove from oven. Remove the brandy snaps from the tray and allow to cool for 1 minute. Gently roll each snap around the handle of a wooden spoon. Allow to cool on the handle for 2–3 minutes, then transfer to wire racks.

❖ To make the pastry cream, whisk the egg yolks and sugar in a bowl until pale. Sift in the flour and mix well. Heat the milk to boiling point and gradually whisk it into the yolk mixture. Pour this mixture back into the saucepan and stir over low heat until the mixture is thick, about 7–10 minutes. Stir in the vanilla. Cool, then pipe mixture into the prepared brandy snaps.

rum & spice cookies

makes about 60

Try brandy in place of the rum or, for a non-alcoholic version, substitute 3 tablespoons water and 2 teaspoon rum extract (essence) for the rum.

¾ cup (6 oz/185 g) butter or margarine, softened

1 cup (8 oz/250 g) superfine (caster) sugar, plus ⅓ cup (3 oz/90 g) extra

1 teaspoon baking powder

½ teaspoon baking soda (bicarbonate of soda)

½ teaspoon ground allspice, plus ¾ teaspoon extra

1 egg

¼ cup (2 fl oz/60 ml) honey

3 tablespoons rum

2⅔ cups (11 oz/340 g) all-purpose (plain) flour

ground allspice

❖ Preheat an oven to 375°F (190°C/Gas Mark 4). Lightly butter baking sheets, or line them with parchment (baking) paper.

❖ In a large mixing bowl beat the butter or margarine with an electric mixer on medium to high speed for 30 seconds. Add the 1 cup sugar, the baking powder, baking soda, and the ½ teaspoon allspice; beat until combined. Beat in the egg, honey, and rum. Beat in as much of the flour as you can with the mixer. Stir in any remaining flour with a wooden spoon. Divide the dough in half. Wrap in plastic wrap and chill for 1 hour, or until dough can be shaped into logs.

❖ In a 9-inch (23-cm) pie plate, stir together the ⅓ cup sugar and ¾ teaspoon allspice. Shape each half of dough into an 8-inch (20-cm) log; roll each log in the sugar–allspice mixture to coat. Wrap in waxed paper or plastic wrap. Chill for 2 hours, or until firm. Cover and reserve remaining sugar and spice mixture.

❖ With a sharp knife and using a sawing motion, cut the chilled dough into ¼-inch (6-mm) thick slices. Place the slices about 2 inches (5 cm) apart on the prepared baking sheets. Sprinkle with the reserved sugar–allspice mixture. Bake for 8–10 minutes, or until edges are firm and bottoms are lightly browned. Remove cookies with a spatula and transfer to a wire rack to cool.

anise butterflies

makes about 60

Making spritz cookies will go more smoothly if you pack the dough firmly into the cookie press. This eliminates any air pockets that could leave holes in the shapes. For more information on making spritz cookies, see pages 298–299.

¾ cup (6 oz/185 g) butter or margarine, softened

½ cup (3½ oz/105 g) packed brown sugar

½ teaspoon baking powder

¼ teaspoon ground cinnamon

⅛ teaspoon ground ginger

1 egg yolk

1 teaspoon anise extract (essence)

2 cups (8 oz/250 g) all-purpose (plain) flour

❖ Preheat an oven to 375°F (190°C/Gas Mark 4).

❖ In a large mixing bowl beat the butter or margarine with an electric mixer on medium to high speed for 30 seconds. Add the brown sugar, baking powder, cinnamon, and ginger; beat until combined. Beat in the egg yolk and anise extract. Beat in as much of the flour as you can with the mixer. Stir in any remaining flour with a wooden spoon. (Do not chill the dough, or it will be too stiff to force through the cookie press.)

❖ Pack the dough into a cookie press fitted with a butterfly plate. Force the dough through the press onto ungreased baking sheets, spacing the cookies 1 inch (2.5 cm) apart.

❖ Bake for 8–10 minutes, or until the edges of the cookies are firm but not brown. Using a spatula, remove from baking sheets and transfer to wire racks to cool.

ladyfingers

makes about 36

**These dainty and versatile
sponge cakes can be made
into sandwiches with jam,
used to line a dessert mold
or as the basis for tiramisu,
or simply served with fresh
fruit and a cup of tea.**

4 egg whites

*½ cup (2 oz/60 g) sifted confectioners' (icing) sugar,
plus 4 teaspoons extra for sprinkling*

4 egg yolks

1 teaspoon vanilla extract

¾ cup (2½ oz/75 g) all purpose (plain) flour

❖ Preheat an oven to 350°F (180°C/Gas Mark 4). If using ladyfinger molds, lightly butter them; or line a baking sheet with parchment (baking) paper or greaseproof paper.

❖ In a large mixing bowl let the egg whites stand at room temperature for 30 minutes. Beat the egg whites with an electric mixer on high speed until soft peaks form (tips curl when beaters are lifted out of the mixture). Gradually add 1 oz (30 g) of the confectioners' sugar, beating until stiff peaks form (tips stand up when beaters are lifted out of the mixture).

❖ In a small mixing bowl beat the egg yolks on medium speed for 1 minute. Gradually add the remaining 1 oz (30 g) confectioners' sugar, beating on high speed until thick and lemon-colored, 4–5 minutes. Stir in the vanilla. Use a metal spoon to gently fold the egg yolk mixture into the egg whites, taking care not to deflate the mixture. Gradually fold in flour. Spoon the batter into a piping bag fitted with a large, round nozzle (about ½ inch/12 mm in diameter). Pipe 3½ x ¾-inch (9 x 2-cm) strips of batter 1 inch (2.5 cm) apart on the prepared baking sheet. (Or, spoon batter into lightly greased ladyfinger molds until batter is even with top of pan.) Sift the 4 teaspoons confectioners' sugar over the top.

❖ Bake for 8–10 minutes, or until lightly browned. Transfer cookies on paper or in ladyfinger molds to a wire rack; cool for about 10 minutes. Remove ladyfingers from the paper or molds, then transfer to the wire rack and allow to cool completely on the rack. Use immediately or store in the freezer.

molasses & ginger stars

makes about 60

These spicy, crisp cookies are perfect for autumn picnics. Look for candied ginger in the spice section at your supermarket, or at gourmet food shops.

1 cup (8 oz/250 g) butter or margarine, softened

²/₃ cup (5 oz/155 g) packed brown sugar

1 tablespoon very finely chopped candied (crystallized) ginger or 1 teaspoon ground ginger

½ teaspoon baking soda (bicarbonate of soda)

¼ cup (2 fl oz/60 ml) light molasses or golden syrup

⅓ cup (3 fl oz/80 ml) milk

3½ cups (14 oz/440 g) all-purpose (plain) flour

ICING

3 cups (12 oz/375 g) confectioners' (icing) sugar

2–3 tablespoons milk

❖ Preheat an oven to 375°F (190°C/Gas Mark 4). Lightly butter baking sheets.

❖ For the dough, in a large mixing bowl beat the butter or margarine with an electric mixer on medium to high speed for 30 seconds. Add the brown sugar, candied or ground ginger, and baking soda; beat until combined. Beat in the molasses or golden syrup and milk. Beat in as much of the flour as you can with the mixer. Stir in any remaining flour with a wooden spoon. Divide the dough in half. Cover and chill for 3 hours, or until easy to handle.

❖ On a lightly floured surface, roll out each half of dough to a ¼-inch (6-mm) thickness. Using a 2-inch (5-cm) star cutter, cut dough into star shapes. Place cookies 1 inch (2.5 cm) apart on prepared baking sheets.

❖ Bake for 7–9 minutes, or until edges are firm. Using a spatula, remove cookies from the baking sheets and transfer to a wire rack to cool.

❖ Meanwhile, for the icing, in a medium mixing bowl stir together the confectioners' sugar and enough of the milk to make an icing of drizzling consistency. Drizzle icing over cookies.

spiced madeleines

makes about 30

These French tea cookies resemble tiny sponge cakes, yet they are not baked in a cake pan. Instead they are formed in small, shell-shaped molds that each produce one portion. Traditional madeleine molds are made out of tinned steel and are available in department stores or specialty cookware stores.

⅔ cup (5 oz/155 g) butter

2 eggs

⅔ cup (5 oz/155 g) superfine (caster) sugar

1¼ cups (5 oz/155 g) all-purpose (plain) flour

½ teaspoon baking powder

1 teaspoon ground cinnamon

¼ teaspoon ground nutmeg

confectioners' (icing) sugar

❖ Preheat an oven to 450°F (220°C/Gas Mark 6). Lightly butter 30 small madeleine molds, then dust them lightly with flour, shaking out any excess. Omit this step if using nonstick molds.

❖ Melt the butter and let it cool slightly. In a bowl, whisk the eggs and sugar until thick and pale. Sift in half the combined sifted flour and baking powder. Fold in gently with a large metal spoon. Pour half the butter round the sides of the bowl and fold in. Repeat with the remaining flour and baking powder, then with the remaining butter. Do not overmix.

❖ Leave to stand for 5 minutes. Place spoonfuls in the molds, filling them to just level with the top. Bake until firm and golden, 8–10 minutes. Cool for 2–3 minutes in the molds, then carefully remove and transfer to a wire rack to cool completely.

❖ Just before serving, sift confectioners' sugar lightly over the tops of the madeleines.

recipe hint

Leaving the batter to stand for 5 minutes before baking helps prevent the madeleines from sticking to the molds.

Madeleines are best baked as close as possible to serving, as they do not keep well.

chocolate madeleines

makes 24 large or 48 small

Madeleines were invented in the French town of Commercy. They were made famous by the French writer Marcel Proust in his novel *Remembrance of Things Past*. The narrator is drinking a cup of tea into which he has dipped a madeleine when suddenly he is flooded with memories of his past.

2/3 cup (5 oz/155 g) butter

2 eggs

2/3 cup (5 oz/155 g) superfine (caster) sugar

1 tablespoon unsweetened cocoa powder

1 1/4 cups (5 oz/155 g) all-purpose (plain) flour

1/2 teaspoon baking powder

confectioners' (icing) sugar or unsweetened cocoa powder, sifted

❖ Preheat an oven to 450°F (220°C/Gas Mark 6). Lightly butter 24 large or 48 small madeleine molds, then dust them lightly with flour, shaking out any excess. Omit this step if using nonstick molds.

❖ Melt the butter and let It cool sllghtly. In a bowl, whlsk the eggs and sugar untll thick and pale. Sift in half the combined sifted cocoa, flour, and baking powder. Fold in gently with a large metal spoon. Pour half the butter round the sides of the bowl and fold in. Repeat with the remaining flour, cocoa, and baking powder, then with the remaining butter. Do not overmix.

❖ Leave to stand for 5 minutes. Place spoonfuls in the molds, filling them to just level with the top. Bake until firm and golden, 8–10 minutes. Cool for 2–3 minutes in the molds, then carefully remove and transfer to a wire rack to cool completely.

❖ Just before serving, sift confectioners' sugar or cocoa powder lightly over the tops of the madeleines.

ginger crisps

makes 25

½ cup (4 oz/125 g) butter

1 tablespoon cornsyrup or golden syrup

1½ cups (6 oz/185 g) self-rising flour

¼ teaspoon baking soda (bicarbonate of soda)

1 teaspoon ground ginger

⅓ cup (3 oz/90 g) packed brown sugar

❖ Preheat an oven to 375°F (190°C/Gas Mark 5). Lightly butter baking sheets, or line them with parchment (baking) paper.

❖ In a saucepan over low heat, gently melt the butter and syrup; be careful not to boil it.

❖ In a bowl, sift the flour, baking soda, and ginger. Add the sugar and the butter mixture to the dry ingredients and mix well.

❖ Form the mixture into 1-inch (2.5-cm) balls and place them on the prepared baking sheets, spacing them well apart. Bake for 12–15 minutes. Let cool on trays for 5 minutes, then transfer to a wire rack to cool completely.

molasses spice
cookies

makes about 24

1/2 cup (4 oz/125 g) butter

1 cup (8 oz/250 g) superfine (caster) sugar

1 egg

1/4 cup (2 fl oz/60 ml) molasses

2 1/2 cups (10 oz/315 g) all-purpose (plain) flour

2 teaspoons baking soda (bicarbonate of soda)

1 teaspoon cinnamon

3/4 teaspoon ground cloves

3/4 teaspoon ground ginger

1/4 teaspoon salt

❖ Preheat an oven to 375°F (190°C/Gas Mark 5). Lightly butter baking sheets, or line them with parchment (baking) paper.

❖ Using an electric mixer on medium to high speed, beat together the butter, sugar, egg, and molasses.

❖ Sift together the flour, baking soda, cinnamon, cloves, ginger, and salt. Add to the butter mixture and mix until thoroughly combined. With lightly wetted hands, form the mixture into 1-inch (2.5-cm) balls and place them 2 inches (5 cm) apart on the prepared baking sheets.

❖ Bake for 10 minutes or until brown. Using a spatula, transfer to wire racks to cool.

gingernuts

makes about 50

These dense-textured cookies have a distinct gingery tang. Stored in an airtight container, they will keep for weeks.

2 cups (8 oz/250 g) all-purpose (plain) flour

1 cup (8 oz/250 g) superfine (caster) sugar, plus extra for sprinkling

½ teaspoon baking soda (bicarbonate of soda)

1 teaspoon cinnamon

2 teaspoons ground ginger

pinch salt

½ cup (4 oz/125 g) cold butter or margarine, cubed

1 small egg

1 tablespoon cornsyrup or golden syrup

superfine (caster) sugar, for sprinkling

❖ Preheat an oven to 300°F (150°C/Gas Mark 3). Lightly butter baking sheets, or line them with parchment (baking) paper.

❖ Into a large bowl, sift together the flour, sugar, baking soda, cinnamon, ginger, and salt. Using your fingertips, rub in the butter or margarine until mixture resembles fine breadcrumbs.

❖ Beat together the egg and syrup and add to the dry ingredients. Using your hands, mix to a firm dough.

❖ Roll the mixture into small balls each about half the size of a walnut. Sprinkle lightly with some of the extra sugar. Place on the prepared baking sheets about 2 inches (5 cm) apart. Bake for 15 minutes or until lightly colored. Using a spatula, loosen the cookies, then allow them to cool on the trays.

sugar glazed
vanilla cookies

makes about 40

These cookies contain a minimum of ingredients, so use the best ingredients—butter, not margarine, and real, not imitation, vanilla extract—to ensure the most delicious flavor.

1/3 cup (3 oz/90 g) butter

1/2 cup (4 oz/125 g) superfine (caster) sugar

1 teaspoon vanilla extract (essence)

1 egg, beaten

1 1/4 cup (5 oz/155 g) self-rising flour, sifted

SUGAR GLAZE

1 tablespoon superfine (caster) sugar

2 tablespoons hot water

❖ Preheat an oven to 350°F (180°C/Gas Mark 4). Lightly butter baking sheets.

❖ Cream the butter, sugar, and vanilla until light and fluffy. Add the beaten egg and mix well. Using a wooden spoon, stir in the flour.

❖ Place the mixture into a piping bag fitted with a plain or fluted nozzle and pipe S shapes, each about 1½ inches (4 cm) long, onto the prepared baking sheets. Lightly brush each cookie with the sugar glaze.

❖ For the sugar glaze, combine the sugar and water in a heatproof bowl, and stir until the sugar is dissolved.

❖ Bake until lightly browned, 12–15 minutes. Using a spatula, loosen immediately, then allow to cool on the baking sheets.

❖ Serve with desserts or coffee.

food facts

Vanilla is derived from the pod of a tropical orchid, *Vanilla planifolia*. The best vanilla pods are expensive, but they last a long time. If they are kept in a jar of sugar, they will imbue the sugar with their flavor; the sugar can then be used in cakes, cookies, and desserts.

Vanilla extract (essence) is made by extracting the flavor from the pods with alcohol. Synthetic vanilla flavors are also available, but they are inferior to the real extract.

citrus
cookies

orange
cheesecake
dreams

makes about 36

**A light orange flavor gives
these individual cheesecakes
a pleasing tang.
If you're making them
for a party, garnish each
square with a thin half
slice of orange.**

CRUST

2 cups (6 oz/185 g) finely crushed vanilla wafers

1/3 cup (3 oz/90 g) butter or margarine, melted

FILLING

1 1/2 cups (11 oz/340 g) cream cheese, softened

3/4 cup (6 oz/185 g) granulated sugar

2 teaspoons finely shredded orange zest (rind)

2 eggs

1/3 cup (3 fl oz/90 ml) orange juice

orange cheesecake dreams

❖ Preheat an oven to 350°F (180°C/Gas Mark 4). Line the base and sides of a 13 x 9 x 2-inch (33 x 23 x 5-cm) baking pan with parchment (baking) paper.

❖ For crust, in a medium mixing bowl stir together the wafer crumbs and melted butter or margarine. Reserve one fourth of the crumb mixture. Press the remaining mixture evenly into the bottom of the prepared pan. Bake for 15 minutes. Allow to cool before adding the filling.

❖ For filling, in another mixing bowl beat the cream cheese with an electric mixer on medium to high speed for 30 seconds. Beat in the sugar and orange zest until combined. Beat in the eggs and orange juice on low speed just until combined. Do not overbeat. Spread the cream cheese mixture evenly over the cooled, baked crust. Sprinkle with the reserved crumb mixture.

❖ Bake for 30–35 minutes, or until the center of the filling appears set. Cool in the pan on a wire rack. Cut into 36 bars or squares. Cover and store in the refrigerator.

microwave orange sauce

makes about 2 cups

(16 fl oz/500 ml)

1 tablespoon cornstarch
(cornflour)

¼ cup (2 fl oz/60 ml) water

2 large oranges

¼ cup (1 oz/30 g) brown sugar

1 tablespoon Grand Marnier or
other orange liqueur (optional)

❖ In a microwave-safe jug, blend the cornstarch and water to a smooth paste. Squeeze the oranges. Strain the juice into the jug and add the brown sugar. Cook on high (100%) for 2 minutes, stirring every 30 seconds. Continue to cook on high until the sauce is thickened and bubbling. Stir in the liqueur, if using.

❖ Serve hot, at room temperature, or cold.

meringue-topped
lemon thins

makes about 40

The meringue on these dainty, wafer-like cookies makes a wonderfully chewy topping. For hints on making meringues, see pages 302–303.

1 cup (8 oz/250 g) butter or margarine, softened

1/2 cup (4 oz/125 g) superfine (caster) sugar

1 tablespoon finely shredded lemon zest (rind)

1/4 teaspoon baking powder

1/4 teaspoon salt

1/4 teaspoon lemon extract (essence)

2 1/2 cups (10 oz/315 g) all-purpose (plain) flour

2 egg whites

2/3 cup (5 oz/155 g) granulated (white) sugar

1/2 cup (2 oz/60 g) flaked almonds

❖ Preheat an oven to 350°F (180°C/Gas Mark 4).

❖ In a large mixing bowl beat the butter or margarine with an electric mixer on medium to high speed for 30 seconds. Add the ½ cup (4 oz/125 g) sugar, the lemon zest, baking powder, and salt; beat until combined. Beat in the lemon extract. Beat in as much of the flour as you can with the mixer. Stir in any remaining flour with a wooden spoon. Divide the dough in half, cover with plastic wrap, and chill for about 3 hours, or until easy to handle.

❖ Roll out each half of dough between 2 layers of parchment (baking) paper to a ¼-inch (6-mm) thickness. Cut into desired shapes using 2- or 2½-inch (5- or 6-cm) cookie cutters. Place 1 inches (2.5 cm) apart on ungreased baking sheets.

❖ In another mixing bowl beat the egg whites with an electric mixer on medium to high speed until soft peaks form (tips curl when beaters are lifted out of the mixture). Gradually beat in the ⅔ cup (5 oz/155 g) sugar until stiff peaks form (tips stand up straight when beaters are lifted out of the mixture). Spread 1 rounded teaspoon of meringue over each cookie; sprinkle a few flaked almonds over each cookie. (Chill the egg white mixture between preparing each batch of cookies for baking.)

❖ Bake for about 11 minutes, or until the meringue is lightly browned. Remove cookies with a spatula and transfer to a wire rack to cool.

frosted lime
wafers

makes about 50

**Finely shredded lime peel
and lime juice impart an
aromatic, citrus tang to
these delicate wafer biscuits.
They may also be made with
lemons or oranges.**

**Use only the thin colored
peel of these fruits, not the
bitter white pith beneath.**

WAFERS

1 cup (8 oz/250 g) butter or margarine, softened

1 cup (8 oz/250 g) granulated sugar

1/2 teaspoon baking soda (bicarbonate of soda)

1/2 teaspoon finely shredded lime zest (rind) or
1 teaspoon finely shredded lemon zest (rind)

1/3 cup (3 fl oz/80 ml) lime juice or lemon juice

2 1/4 cups (9 oz/280 g) all-purpose (plain) flour

GLAZE

1 cup (4 oz/125 g) sifted confectioners' (icing) sugar

3 tablespoons butter or margarine, softened

1–2 tablespoons lime juice or lemon juice

few drops green or yellow food coloring (optional)

❖ Preheat an oven to 375°F (190°C/Gas Mark 4).

❖ For wafers, in a mixing bowl beat the butter or margarine with an electric mixer on medium to high speed for 30 seconds. Add the sugar, baking soda, and lime or lemon zest; beat until combined. Beat in the lime or lemon juice. Beat in as much of the flour as you can with the mixer. Stir in any remaining flour with a wooden spoon.

❖ Drop rounded teaspoons of dough 2 inches (5 cm) apart onto ungreased baking sheets. Bake for about 10 minutes, or until the edges are beginning to brown. Remove the wafers with a spatula and transfer to a wire rack to cool.

❖ Meanwhile, for glaze, in a small mixing bowl beat together the confectioners' sugar, softened butter or margarine, and enough lime or lemon juice to make a mixture of glazing consistency. If desired, stir in food coloring. Dip the tops of the wafers in the glaze. Place wafers, glazed side up, on wire racks and allow the glaze to set before serving.

lemon-pistachio
pretzels

makes about 50

If you want to make these
sweet pretzels even more
delicate in texture, grind the
nuts in a blender or food
processor instead of
just chopping them.

¾ cup (6 oz/185 g) butter or margarine, softened

1 cup (4 oz/125 g) sifted confectioners' (icing) sugar

2 teaspoons finely shredded lemon zest (rind)

1 egg

½ teaspoon lemon extract (essence)

2¼ cups (9 oz/280 g) all-purpose (plain) flour

1½ cups (6 oz/185 g) sifted confectioners' (icing) sugar

1 tablespoon lemon juice

1–2 tablespoons water

⅓ cup (2 oz/60 g) finely chopped pistachios, walnuts, or almonds

❖ Preheat an oven to 375°F (190°C/Gas Mark 4). Lightly butter baking sheets.

❖ In a mixing bowl beat the butter or margarine with an electric mixer on medium to high speed for 30 seconds. Add the 1 cup (4 oz/125 g) confectioners' sugar and the lemon zest; beat until combined. Beat in the egg and lemon extract. Beat in as much of the flour as you can with the mixer. Stir in any remaining flour with a wooden spoon. Divide the dough in half. If necessary, cover with plastic wrap and chill for 30–60 minutes, or until dough is easy to handle.

❖ On a lightly floured surface, shape each half of the dough into a 12-inch (30-cm) log. Cut each log into twenty-four ½-inch (12-mm) pieces. Roll each piece into an 8-inch (20-cm) rope. Form each rope into a pretzel shape by crossing one end over the other, forming a circle in the middle and overlapping ends by about 1 inch (2.5 cm). Bring the ends down to the opposite edge of the circle and press lightly to seal. Place pretzels about 2 inches (5 cm) apart on the prepared baking sheets.

❖ Bake for 8–10 minutes, or until golden brown. Remove with a spatula and transfer to a wire rack to cool.

❖ In a small bowl stir together the 1½ cups (6 oz/185 g) confectioners' sugar, the lemon juice, and enough water to make a mixture of glazing consistency. Brush cookies with the glaze, then sprinkle with pistachios or other nuts. Let stand until the glaze is set.

citrus shortbread

makes 8 or 16

The simplicity of shortbread
lends itself well to
variations. In this version,
the buttery richness of the
dough is offset by the fresh
tang of citrus.

1 cup (4 oz/125 g) all-purpose (plain) flour

1/3 cup (3 oz/90 g) granulated (white) sugar

1/8 teaspoon salt

2 teaspoons finely shredded lemon or orange zest (rind)

1/2 cup (4 oz/125 g) cold butter

1/4 teaspoon lemon or orange extract (essence)

nonstick cooking spray or vegetable oil

sifted confectioners' (icing) sugar (optional)

❖ Preheat an oven to 325°F (165°C/Gas Mark 3).

❖ In a medium mixing bowl stir together the flour, sugar, salt, and lemon or orange zest. Cut in the butter until the mixture resembles fine crumbs. Sprinkle with the lemon or orange extract. Form the mixture into a ball and knead lightly and briefly until smooth. Do not overknead, as this will make the shortbread tough.

❖ The shortbread can be made with or without a wooden or ceramic shortbread mold. If using a mold, spray it with nonstick baking spray or brush it lightly and thoroughly with oil. Firmly press the dough into the mold. Invert the mold over a lightly greased baking sheet and tap the mold lightly to release the dough over the baking sheet. (If necessary, use a knife to pry the dough out of the mold.)

❖ Alternatively, pat the dough into an 8-inch (20-cm) circle on a lightly greased baking sheet. With a fork, prick the dough deeply. Score into 8 or 16 wedges with the back of a knife.

❖ Bake for about 25 minutes, or until the center of the shortbread is set. While it is still warm, cut the molded shortbread into wedges or cut hand-shaped shortbread along the perforations; remove the shortbread from the baking sheet and transfer to a wire rack to cool. If desired, sprinkle wedges with sifted confectioners' sugar just before serving.

orange marmalade wreaths

makes about 20

Dress up these wreaths by drizzling melted chocolate over them. For the Christmas season, press snipped pieces of red and green maraschino (glacé) cherries into the drizzled chocolate while it is still warm.

COOKIES

1 cup (8 oz/250 g) butter or margarine, softened

¾ cup (3 oz/90 g) sifted confectioners' (icing) sugar

2 teaspoons grated orange zest (rind)

2 cups (8 oz/250 g) all-purpose (plain) flour

FILLING

⅓ cup (3 oz/90 g) cream cheese, softened

2 tablespoons orange marmalade

DRIZZLE (OPTIONAL)

¼ cup (1½ oz/45 g) semisweet (plain) chocolate, chopped

½ teaspoon solid vegetable shortening

❖ Preheat an oven to 375°F (190°C/Gas Mark 4).

❖ For cookies, in a large mixing bowl beat the butter or margarine with an electric mixer on medium to high speed for 30 seconds. Add the confectioners' sugar and orange zest; beat until combined. Beat in as much of the flour as you can with the mixer. Stir in any remaining flour with a wooden spoon. Do not chill the dough.

❖ Pack the dough into a cookie press fitted with a wreath plate. Force the dough through the cookie press onto ungreased baking sheets to form wreath shapes spaced 1 inch (2.5 cm) apart.

❖ Bake for 7–9 minutes, or until edges are firm but not brown. Remove cookies with a spatula and transfer to a wire rack to cool.

❖ For filling, in a small mixing bowl stir together the cream cheese and orange marmalade. Spread 1 teaspoon of the mixture over the flat side of half the cookies; top with remaining cookies, flat sides down.

❖ If desired, for drizzle, in a small, heavy saucepan melt chocolate and shortening over low heat. Drizzle over cookies.

microwave lemon butter

makes about 3 lb (1.5 kg)

½ cup (4 oz/125 g) butter

2 cups (1 lb/500 g) sugar

6 eggs, at room temperature

finely grated zest and juice of 4 large lemons

❖ In a 1–2 quart (1.5–2 l) microwave-safe dish, melt the butter on high (100 %) for 2 minutes. Meanwhile, using an electric mixer, beat the sugar, eggs, lemon zest, and juice until thoroughly combined. Gradually whisk in the melted butter. Cook on high for 8 minutes, stirring every 2 minutes, until the mixture thickens and coats the back of a spoon.

❖ If not using immediately, pour the hot lemon butter into warmed, sterilized jars, seal, and label. If using immediately, allow to cool, then use to sandwich Melting Moments (page 92), or to accompany Ginger Brownies (page 54) or Almond Biscotti (page 246–247).

❖ Unopened jars of lemon butter will keep for up to 4 weeks. Refrigerate after opening. Once opened, use within 7 days.

orange spice bars

makes 12–15

1½ cups (6 oz/185 g) self-rising flour

½ cup (3½ oz/105 g) firmly packed brown sugar

½ teaspoon ground ginger

½ teaspoon ground cinnamon

½ teaspoon ground nutmeg

2 teaspoons finely grated orange zest (rind)

½ cup (4 oz/125 g) butter or margarine

1 tablespoons honey

¼ cup (2 oz/60 g) sliced (flaked) almonds

❖ Preheat an oven to 375°F (190°C/Gas Mark 4). Lightly butter an 11 x 7-inch (28 x 18-cm) cake pan.

❖ In a bowl, combine the flour, sugar, ginger, cinnamon, nutmeg, and orange zest.

❖ In a saucepan, combine the butter or margarine and honey and melt over low heat. Add to the dry ingredients and mix well.

❖ Press the mixture into the prepared pan and top with the almonds. Bake for about 20 minutes or until lightly golden. Allow to cool for a few minutes, then cut into 12–15 squares and leave in the tin to cool completely.

fruit
cookies

dried fruit
cookies

makes about 50

If desired, substitute 2½ cups of prepared mix containing dried fruit, nuts, and coconut for the fruits, coconut, and chopped nuts required in this recipe. Be sure to break up any banana chips and whole nuts, and snip any other large pieces of dried fruit into bits.

¾ cup (6 oz/185 g) butter or margarine, softened

½ cup (4 oz/125 g) granulated (white) sugar

½ cup (3½ oz/105 g) packed brown sugar

1 teaspoon baking powder

½ teaspoon baking soda (bicarbonate of soda)

1 teaspoon ground allspice

2 eggs

1 cup (3 medium) mashed bananas

1 teaspoon vanilla extract (essence)

2 cups (8 oz/250 g) all-purpose (plain) flour

1½ cups (4½ oz/140 g) rolled oats

1 cup (6 oz/185 g) mixed dried fruit, chopped

¾ cup (2½ oz/75 g) shredded dried coconut

¾ cup (3 oz/90 g) chopped peanuts, walnuts, or pecans

dried fruit cookies

❖ Preheat an oven to 375°F (190°C/Gas Mark 4).

❖ In a large mixing bowl beat the butter or margarine with an electric mixer on medium to high speed for 30 seconds. Add the granulated sugar, brown sugar, baking powder, baking soda, and allspice; beat until combined. Beat in the eggs, mashed bananas, and vanilla. Beat in as much of the flour as you can with the mixer. Stir in any remaining flour with a wooden spoon. Stir in the oats, dried fruit, coconut, and nuts.

❖ Drop rounded tablespoons of dough 2 inches (5 cm) apart onto ungreased baking sheets. Bake for 10–12 minutes, or until golden brown. Using a spatula, remove the cookies and transfer to wire racks to cool.

recipe hint

To prevent the banana from going brown, add 1 teaspoon lemon juice to the banana while you are mashing it.

panforte

makes 16–20 wedges

Panforte is Italian for "strong bread"— a good description of this honey-flavored confection laden with fruit and nuts. It lends itself well to variations with different types and proportions of fruit and nuts; just keep the total weight of fruit and nuts the same. Serve thin wedges with tea or coffee.

1 cup (4 oz/125 g) flaked (slivered) almonds

1 cup (4 oz/125 g) coarsely chopped roasted hazelnuts

2 oz (60 g) candied (glacé) apricots, chopped

2 oz/60 g candied (glacé) orange peel, chopped

2 oz/60 g candied (glacé) pineapple, chopped

2 oz/60 g candied (glacé) figs, chopped

5 oz (155 g) semisweet (plain) chocolate, chopped

2/3 cup (2¾ oz/80 g) all-purpose (plain) flour

2 tablespoons unsweetened cocoa powder

1 teaspoon ground cinnamon

1/3 cup (3 oz/90 g) sugar

2/3 cup (8 fl oz/250 ml) honey

confectioners' (icing) sugar

panforte

❖ Preheat an oven to 350°F (180°C/Gas Mark 4). Butter an 8-inch (20-cm) round cake pan and line it with parchment (baking) paper or edible rice paper.

❖ Mix together the almonds, hazelnuts, apricots, orange peel, pineapple, figs, one-third of the chocolate, the flour, cocoa, and cinnamon in a bowl until combined.

❖ Combine the remaining chocolate, the sugar, and honey in a pan and stir over low heat until melted. Bring to a boil and simmer for 1 minute.

❖ Pour the hot liquid mixture into the fruit and nut mixture. Using a wooden spoon, stir quickly to combine. Spread the mixture into the prepared pan, pressing it down firmly and evenly with the back of a spoon or with lightly wetted hands, being careful not to burn yourself on the hot toffee mixture. Bake for 35 minutes, or until firm. Cool for 10 minutes in the pan before turning out onto a wire rack. If the mixture seems to be sticking to the pan, run a blunt-ended knife around the edge of the pan to loosen the panforte. Serve cut into thin wedges and dusted with sifted confectioners' (icing) sugar.

eccles cakes

1 cup (6 oz/185 g) currants

½ cup (3 oz/90 g) mixed peel

1 tablespoon brandy

½ teaspoon ground cinnamon

1 tablespoon superfine (caster) sugar plus 2 teaspoons extra, for sprinkling

3 sheets ready-rolled purchased puff pastry

1 egg white, lightly beaten

❖ Preheat an oven to 400°F (200°C/Gas Mark 5). Lightly butter baking sheets.

❖ For the filling, in a bowl combine the currants, peel, brandy, cinnamon and 1 tablespoon sugar.

❖ With a plain or fluted cutter, cut nine 3-inch (7.5-cm) rounds from each sheet of pastry. Place 2 teaspoons of filling on each round. Bring the edges of the pastry up, press them together, and pinch the seams to seal. Turn the pastries seam side down and roll them into ½-inch (12-mm) thick rounds or ovals.

❖ Place the pastries on the prepared trays. Brush with egg white and sprinkle with the extra sugar. Make 3 slashes across the top of each cake. Bake for 15–20 minutes, or until golden. Transfer to wire racks to cool.

prune puffs

makes about 30

This Italian dessert used to be fried in very hot oil or melted pork fat, but today a more healthful alternative is to bake it in a hot oven. Puff pastry can be bought already prepared, or filo pastry may be substituted. If using frozen pastry, allow it to thaw before proceeding with the recipe.

6 oz (180 g) prunes

½ bottle (190 ml) white dessert wine

1 small piece of lemon zest (rind)

3 tablespoons superfine (caster) sugar, plus extra for sprinkling

10 oz (300 g) puff pastry or filo pastry

1 tablespooon (½ oz/15 g) butter, melted

❖ Preheat an oven to 350°F (180°C/Gas Mark 4). Lightly butter a baking sheet.

❖ In a bowl, soak the prunes in the wine for several hours. Drain, reserving the wine. Place the prunes in a saucepan. Add the lemon zest, sugar, and ½ cup (4 fl oz/125 ml) of the reserved wine. Cover and cook over low heat for about 15 minutes. Drain the prunes and pit (stone) them. Set aside.

❖ Roll out the pastry to a fairly thin sheet. Using a cookie cutter, cut it into 4-inch (10-cm) circles. Brush the edge of each circle with water. Place a prune on each pastry disk, fold the dough over it, and press the edges of the dough to seal. Prick with a fork or make a small slit in the center with a knife. This allows the steam to escape and the pastry to puff.

❖ Place the prune puffs on the prepared baking sheet. Brush the tops of the pastries with melted butter and sprinkle each with a little superfine sugar. Bake for 20 minutes, or until golden. Serve hot, warm, or at room temperature.

date and oat slices

makes 12

Thse wholesome treats are easy to make and have a sturdy texture, so they're good to take along on picnics or to put in the kids' school lunchboxes.

1/2 lb (250 g) pitted dates, chopped

3 oz (90 g) firmly packed brown sugar

1/2 cup (4 fl oz/125 ml) water

few drops vanilla extract (essence)

1 cup (4 oz/125 g) self-rising flour

1 teaspoon baking soda (bicarbonate of soda)

1/2 cup (4 oz/125 g) butter or margarine

1 1/3 cup (4 oz/125 g) rolled oats

❖ Preheat an oven to 375°F (190°C/Gas Mark 5). Lightly butter a 7 x 11 x 1½ inch/ 18 x 28 x 4 cm cake pan.

❖ Place the dates, 1 oz (30 g) of the sugar, and the water in a saucepan. Bring to the boil, then reduce the heat to low and simmer for about 8 minutes or until the dates are softened and the water is nearly all absorbed. Add the vanilla.

❖ In a bowl, sift the flour and baking soda. Using your fingertips, lightly rub in the butter or margarine until the mixture resembles breadcrumbs, then stir in the oats.

❖ Press half of the oat mixture over the base of the prepared tin. Spread it with the date filling. Top with the remaining oat mixture, pressing down lightly with wetted fingers.

❖ Bake for 25–30 minutes or until the top is lightly browned.

❖ Cool slightly, then cut into slices in the tin. Allow to cool completely before lifting the slices out of the tin.

ricotta foldovers

makes 30

**in this Italian recipe, a rich,
buttery cookie dough
encloses a sweetened ricotta
filling. These pastries—
known in Italian as *piconi
marchigiani*, or "stuffed
pastries from the marshes"—
are served in their homeland
as dessert, breakfast food,
or for afternoon tea.**

PASTRY

2 cups (8 oz/250 g) all-purpose (plain) flour

3 egg yolks, beaten

½ cup (4 oz/125 g) butter, chopped and softened

¾ cup (6 oz/185 g) superfine (caster) sugar

1 teaspoon grated lemon zest (rind)

cold water as needed

FILLING

2 egg yolks

1 cup (8 oz/250 g) sugar

pinch of ground cinnamon

grated zest (rind) of 1 lemon

1 teaspoon rum (optional)

3 oz (90 g) semisweet (plain) chocolate, grated

3 oz (90 g) almonds, ground

1 lb (500 g) ricotta

Confectioners' (icing) sugar, for dusting (optional)

❖ Preheat an oven to 300°F (150°C/Gas Mark 2). Lightly butter a baking sheet.

❖ The pastry can be made by hand or in a food processor. If making it by hand, heap the flour on a work surface and make a well in the center. In the well, place the egg yolks, butter, sugar, and lemon zest. Knead quickly to make a medium-soft dough, adding a little cold water if needed to bring the dough together. If making it in a food processor, place the flour, egg yolks, butter, sugar, and lemon zest in the bowl of the processor and process, using the pulse button, until the pastry comes together, adding a little cold water if necessary. Roll the pastry into a ball, wrap in plastic wrap, and place in the refrigerator to chill for 1 hour.

❖ For the filling, in a bowl, beat the egg yolks. Reserve about 1 tablespoon to use for brushing the pastries; set aside. To the remaining egg yolks, add the sugar, cinnamon, lemon zest, rum (if using), chocolate, and almonds. Beat until well combined. The mixture should be thick.

❖ Roll out the dough to a 1/16-inch (1 mm) thickness. Using a cookie cutter, cut into 3-inch (8-cm) rounds. Prick with a fork or make a small slit in the center of each foldover to allow steam to escape. Place 1 teaspoon of the filling in the center of each round and fold the dough over into a half-moon shape, pressing with your fingers to seal the edges well.

❖ Place on the baking sheet and brush the foldovers with the reserved beaten egg. Bake until a toothpick inserted in the center of a pastry comes out clean and dry, about 20 minutes.

❖ Transfer to wire racks to cool. Serve warm or at room temperature. If desired, dust with a little confectioners' sugar just before serving.

pumpkin swirls

makes about 12

These unusual pastry-like treats resemble doughnuts. We've made them into 3-inch (7.5-cm) swirl shapes, but they can be piped into any shape you desire.

2 cups (8 oz/250 g) all-purpose (plain) flour

1/2 cup (3 1/2 oz/105 g) packed brown sugar

1 1/2 teaspoons baking powder

1 1/2 teaspoons pumpkin pie spice or mixed spice

1/2 teaspoon salt

1/4 teaspoon baking soda (bicarbonate of soda)

1/2 cup (4 oz/125 g) canned pumpkin or home-cooked mashed pumpkin

1 egg

1/4 cup (2 fl oz/60 ml) milk

1/4 cup (2 oz/60 g) butter, or margarine, softened

ICING

1 cup (4 oz/125 g) sifted confectioners' (icing) sugar

1/4 teaspoon vanilla extract (essence)

3–4 teaspoons milk

❖ Preheat an oven to 375°F (190°F/Gas Mark 4).
Lightly butter 2 baking sheets.

❖ For doughnuts, in a medium mixing bowl stir
together the flour, brown sugar, baking powder,
pumpkin pie spice, salt, and baking soda. Add the
pumpkin, eggs, milk, and butter or margarine; beat
with an electric mixer on low speed until mixed.

❖ Spoon the mixture into a pastry bag fitted with a
large star tip with a 2-inch (5-cm) opening. Pipe onto
prepared baking sheets in 3-inch (7.5-cm) circles. Bake
for 10 minutes, or until golden brown.

❖ With a spatula, transfer the doughnuts to a wire
rack lined with waxed paper to cool. Leave until
completely cool before icing.

❖ For icing, in a small mixing bowl stir together the
confectioners' sugar and vanilla. Stir in enough milk to
make a smooth icing of glazing consistency. Spoon
icing over doughnuts.

recipe variation

In place of the icing, try
sprinkling the swirls with
a mixture of 2 tablespoons
granulated sugar and
½ teaspoon pumpkin pie
spice before baking.

apricot crunch

makes 24

2 tablespoons (1½ oz/45 g)
butter or margarine

½ cup (4 oz/125 g) sugar

2 tablespoons self-rising flour

1 egg

½ cup (2 oz/60 g) roughly
chopped dried apricots

1 cup (1½ oz/45 g)
bran flakes cereal

½ cup (2 oz/60 g) roughly
chopped pecans or walnuts

½ cup (2 oz/60 g)
confectioners' (icing) sugar,
sifted

❖ Place the butter or margarine in a large microwave-safe dish. Cook on high (100%) for 45 seconds. Stir in the sugar, flour, egg, and apricots. Cook on high for 2 minutes until the mixture bubbles. Stir well, then stir in the bran flakes and nuts. Mix well until all ingredients are thoroughly combined. Leave the mixture to cool for a few minutes. When cool enough to handle, form into ¾-inch (2-cm) balls.

❖ Place the confectioners' sugar into a plastic bag, then add 3 or 4 balls to the bag. Gently toss to coat the balls with the sugar. Transfer the coated balls to a plate and repeat in batches with the remaining balls. Chill for 2–3 hours before serving.

sour cream date triangles

makes about 36

2¹/₂ cups (10 oz/310 g) all-purpose (plain) flour

1¹/₄ cups (9 oz/270 g) packed brown sugar

1 teaspoon baking powder

1 teaspoon ground cinnamon

¹/₂ teaspoon baking soda (bicarbonate of soda)

¹/₂ teaspoon salt

2 eggs

1 cup (8 oz/250 g) butter, softened

¹/₂ cup (4 fl oz/125 ml) sour cream

1¹/₃ cups (8 oz/250 g) chopped pitted dates or raisins

¹/₂ cup (2 oz/60 g) chopped walnuts or pecans

GLAZE

1¹/₂ cups (6 oz/185 g) sifted confectioners' (icing) sugar

3 tablespoons butter or margarine, melted

1 tablespoon lemon juice

1–2 tablespoons water

few drops yellow food coloring (optional)

sour cream date triangles

❖ Preheat an oven to 350°F (180°C/Gas Mark 4). Lightly butter a 15 x 10 x 1-inch (37.5 x 25 x 2.5-cm) baking pan.

❖ For bars, in a medium mixing bowl stir together the flour, brown sugar, baking powder, cinnamon, baking soda, and salt. Beat in the eggs, butter, and sour cream until thoroughly combined. Stir in the dates or raisins and walnuts or pecans. Spread the batter in the prepared pan.

❖ Bake for 20–25 minutes, or until a wooden toothpick inserted near the center comes out clean. Cool in the pan on a wire rack.

❖ For glaze, in a medium mixing bowl stir together the confectioners' sugar, melted butter or margarine, lemon juice, and enough water to make a mixture of glazing consistency. If desired, tint glaze with food coloring. Spread glaze over cooled bars. Cut into rectangles, then halve rectangles diagonally to make triangles.

recipe variation

In place of the glaze, try icing the triangles with Cream Cheese Icing or Lemon Cream Cheese Icing (page 167).

cream cheese
icings

cream cheese icing

½ cup (4 oz/125 g) cream cheese, softened

2 tablespoons (1 oz/30 g) butter, softened

1½ cups (6 oz/185 g) confectioners' (icing) sugar, sifted

In a bowl, combine the cream cheese, butter, and icing sugar. Using an electric mixer, mix until smooth and fluffy. Using a palette knife or spatula, spread the icing over the top of the cooled brownies or bar cookies.

makes 2 cups (8 oz/500 g)

lemon cream cheese icing

2 tablespoons (1 oz/30 g) butter, softened

2 oz (60 g) cream cheese, softened

1 tablespoon grated lemon zest (rind)

1½ cups (6 oz/185 g) confectioners' (icing) sugar, sifted

In a bowl, combine the butter and cream cheese. Using an electric mixer, mix until creamy. Mix in the lemon zest (rind) and sugar and beat until smooth.Using a palette knife or spatula, spread the icing over the cooled brownies or bar cookies.

makes 2 cups (8 oz/500 g)

carrot raisin drops

makes about 70

If you want the flavor of carrot cake without the fuss, try these moist, cake-like cookies.

1 cup (8 oz/250 g) butter or margarine, softened

1 cup (7 oz/220 g) packed brown sugar

1 teaspoon baking soda (bicarbonate of soda)

1 teaspoon ground cinnamon

1 teaspoon finely shredded orange zest (rind)

1/2 teaspoon ground ginger

1/2 teaspoon ground nutmeg

2 eggs

1 teaspoon vanilla extract

2 cups (8 oz/250 g) all-purpose (plain) flour

1 1/2 cups (6 oz/185 g) finely shredded carrots

1 cup (3 oz/90 g) rolled oats

1 cup (6 oz/185 g) raisins

1/2 cup (2 oz/60 g) chopped walnuts or pecans

❖ Preheat an oven to 375°F (190°C/Gas Mark 4).

❖ In a mixing bowl beat the butter or margarine with an electric mixer on medium to high speed for 30 seconds. Add the brown sugar, baking soda, cinnamon, orange peel, ginger, and nutmeg; beat until combined. Beat in the eggs and vanilla. Beat in as much of the flour as you can with the mixer. Stir in any remaining flour with a wooden spoon. Stir in the carrots, oats, raisins, and nuts.

❖ Drop rounded teaspoons of dough 2 inches (5 cm) apart onto ungreased baking sheets. Bake for 6–8 minutes, or until golden brown. Using a spatula, transfer cookies to wire racks to cool.

recipe variations

For an extra touch of sweetness, spread each cookie with a little of your favorite cream cheese frosting, such as one of the recipes on page 167.

pumpkin spice bars

makes about 50

Don't wait until winter to make these soft bars; they're just as good with a glass of lemonade as with a cup of hot cider. Look for candied (glacé) ginger in supermarkets and gourmet shops.

2 cups (8 oz/250 g) all-purpose (plain) flour

½ cup (3½ oz/105 g) packed brown sugar

½ cup (4 oz/125 g) granulated (white) sugar

2 teaspoons baking powder

¼ teaspoon baking soda (bicarbonate of soda)

2 teaspoons finely chopped candied (glacé) ginger or ½ teaspoon ground ginger

1 teaspoon ground cinnamon

¼ teaspoon salt

2 eggs

1 cup (8 oz/250 g) cooked mashed pumpkin

¾ cup (4½ oz/140 g) raisins

½ cup (4 fl oz/125 ml) vegetable oil

TOPPING

½ cup (3 oz/90 g) white chocolate, chopped

1 teaspoon solid vegetable shortening or butter

❖ Preheat an oven to 350°F (180°C/Gas Mark 4).

❖ For bars, in a large mixing bowl stir together the flour, brown sugar, granulated sugar, baking powder, baking soda, candied or ground ginger, cinnamon, and salt. In another mixing bowl beat the eggs lightly. Stir in the pumpkin, raisins, and oil. Stir the pumpkin mixture into the flour mixture.

❖ Spread the batter into a 15 x 10 x 1-inch (37.5 x 25 x 2.5-cm) baking pan lined with parchment (baking) paper. Bake for 15–20 minutes, or until a wooden toothpick or fine skewer inserted near the center comes out clean. Cool in the pan on a wire rack.

❖ For topping, in a small, heavy-duty plastic bag combine the white chocolate and shortening or butter. Close the bag just above the ingredients, then set the sealed bag in a bowl of warm water until the contents are melted.

❖ Snip ¼ inch (6 mm) from one corner of the bag. Squeeze the topping from the bag over the bars in a crisscross design. Cut the bars into small squares before the topping is completely set.

makes about 36 drops

½ cup (4 oz/125 g) butter or margarine

1 teaspoon ground cinnamon

1 teaspoon finely shredded orange zest (rind)

½ teaspoon baking soda (bicarbonate of soda)

1 egg

½ cup (6 fl oz/185 ml) honey

3 tablespoons orange juice or milk

2¼ cups (9 oz/270 g) all-purpose (plain) flour

1 cup (6 oz/185 g) chopped dried figs, pitted dates, or raisins

ORANGE ICING

1 cup (4 oz/125 g) sifted confectioners' (icing) sugar

1–2 tablespoons orange juice

❖ Preheat an oven to 350°F (180°C/Gas Mark 4).

❖ For drops, in a mixing bowl beat the shortening with an electric mixer on medium to high speed for 30 seconds. Add the cinnamon, orange peel, and baking soda; beat until combined. Beat in the egg, honey, and orange juice or milk until combined. Beat in as much of the flour as you can with the mixer. Stir in any remaining flour with a wooden spoon. Stir in the figs, dates, or raisins.

❖ Drop rounded teaspoons of dough 2 inches (5 cm) apart onto ungreased baking sheets. Bake for 10–12 minutes, or until lightly browned. Remove drops and transfer to wire racks to cool.

❖ Meanwhile, for icing, in a small mixing bowl stir together confectioners' sugar and enough of the orange juice to make an icing of drizzling consistency. Drizzle drops with icing.

orange-fig drops

apricot macaroon
bars

makes about 36 bars

CRUST

¾ cup (6 oz/185 g) butter or margarine, softened

1 cup (8 oz/250 g) granulated (white) sugar

2 eggs

¼ teaspoon almond extract (essence)

1½ cups (6 oz/185 g) all-purpose (plain) flour

1 cup (3 oz/90 g) shredded coconut

FILLING

1½ cups (6 oz/185 g)
dried apricots, chopped

1 cup (8 fl oz/250 ml) water

½ cup (3½ oz/105 g) packed
brown sugar

½ teaspoon vanilla extract

⅓ cup (1 oz/30 g) toasted
shredded coconut

❖ Preheat an oven to 350°F (180°C/Gas Mark 4). Generously butter a 13 x 9 x 2-inch (33 x 23 x 5-cm) baking pan.

❖ For the crust, in a large mixing bowl beat the butter or margarine with an electric mixer on medium to high speed for 30 seconds. Add the granulated sugar and beat until combined. Beat in the eggs and almond extract.

❖ Beat in as much of the flour as you can with the mixer. Stir in any remaining flour with a wooden spoon, then stir in the coconut. Spread the batter into the prepared pan and bake for 25 minutes.

❖ Meanwhile, for the filling, in a saucepan combine the dried apricots and water. Bring to a boil, then reduce the heat, cover, and simmer for 7–8 minutes, or until the apricots are tender. Add the brown sugar and cook, stirring, until dissolved. Remove from the heat and stir in the vanilla. Spoon over the hot crust.

❖ Bake for 10 minutes more, or until a toothpick inserted near the center comes out clean. Remove from the oven and sprinkle evenly with the toasted coconut. Cool in the pan on a rack. Cut into 36 bars.

raspberry–orange
strips

makes about 18 cookies

1 cup (8 oz/250 g) butter, softened

½ cup (3½ oz/105 g) superfine (caster) sugar

1 teaspoon finely shredded orange zest

3 cups (12 oz/375 g) all-purpose (plain) flour

¼ cup (2½ oz/75 g) seedless raspberry jam

½ cup (2 oz/60 g) chopped pistachios, flaked almonds, or pine nuts

❖ Preheat an oven to 325°F (165°C/Gas Mark 3).

❖ In a large mixing bowl beat together the butter, sugar, and orange zest. Add the flour and mix with a flat-bladed knife until the mixture resembles fine crumbs. Form the mixture into a ball and knead briefly until smooth. Divide the dough in half.

❖ Roll each portion into an 8-inch (20-cm) log. Place the logs 4–5 inches (10–12.5 cm) apart on an ungreased baking sheet. Pat each into a 2-inch (5-cm) wide strip. Chill for 30 minutes to firm. Using the back of a spoon, press a 1-inch (2.5-cm) wide indentation lengthwise down the center of each strip. Bake for 20–25 minutes, or until the edges are lightly browned. Transfer the baking sheet to a wire rack. Spoon the jam into the indentations. While still warm, cut the strips on the bias into 1-inch (2.5-cm) wide pieces. Sprinkle with nuts. Leave on baking sheet until completely cool.

fruity foldovers

½ cup (4 oz/125 g) butter or margarine, softened

¼ cup (2 oz/60 g) packed brown sugar

½ teaspoon baking soda (bicarbonate of soda)

½ teaspoon ground coriander

¼ teaspoon salt

1 egg

1 teaspoon vanilla extract

2¼ cups (9 oz/280 g) all-purpose (plain) flour

¼ cup (2 fl oz/60 ml) apple or redcurrant jelly

½ cup (3 oz/90 g) chopped mixed dried fruits (such as apricots, apples, peaches, prunes, dates, or raisins)

⅓ cup (1½ oz/45 g) finely chopped pecans or walnuts

sifted confectioners' (icing) sugar

❖ Preheat an oven to 375°F (190°C/Gas Mark 4).

❖ In a mixing bowl beat the butter or margarine with an electric mixer on medium to high speed for 30 seconds. Add the brown sugar, baking soda, coriander, and salt; beat until combined. Beat in the egg and vanilla. Beat in as much of the flour as you can with the mixer. Stir in any remaining flour with a wooden spoon. Divide the dough in half. Cover and chill for 3 hours, or until it is easy to handle.

❖ Meanwhile, in a small saucepan heat the apple or red-currant jelly until melted. Remove from the heat. Stir in the dried fruit and pecans or walnuts.

❖ On a lightly floured surface roll each half of the dough between two sheets of parchment (baking) paper to a ⅛-inch (3-mm) thickness. Using a 2½-inch (6-cm) round cookie cutter, cut into rounds. Place cookies ½-inch (12 mm) apart on ungreased baking sheets. Spoon 1 teaspoon of the dried fruit mixture onto the center of each round and fold the round in half. Seal cut edges of each round with the tines of a fork.

❖ Bake for 7–9 minutes, or until bottoms are lightly browned. Transfer cookies to a wire rack to cool. Sprinkle lightly with sifted confectioners' sugar.

oatmeal
golden raisin
cookies

makes about 24

1¼ cup (5 oz/155 g)
all-purpose (plain) flour

⅔ cup (5 oz/155 g)
superfine (caster) sugar

1 cup (3 oz/90 g) rolled oats

1 cup (4 oz/125 g)
shredded dried coconut

½ cup (3 oz/90 g) golden
raisins (sultanas)

½ cup (4 oz/125 g)
unsalted butter

2 tablespoons cornsyrup,
light molasses, or golden
syrup

1 teaspoon baking soda
(bicarbonate of soda)

1 tablespoon boiling water

❖ Preheat an oven to 325°F (160°C/Gas Mark 3). Line a large baking tray with parchment (baking) paper.

❖ Sift the flour into a large bowl, then stir in the sugar, rolled oats, coconut, and golden raisins. Make a well in the center.

❖ In a small saucepan melt the butter and syrup over a low heat. In a small bowl dissolve the bicarbonate of soda in the boiling water and add immediately to the butter mixture.

❖ Add the butter mixture to the flour mixture and mix thoroughly.

❖ Place tablespoons of the mixture onto the prepared baking sheet, spacing them about 2 inches (5 cm) apart.

❖ Bake until lightly browned, 15–20 minutes. Cool for 2–3 minutes on the tray then transfer to a wire rack to cool completely.

date sticks

makes 16–20

2 eggs

*¼ cup (2 oz/60 g) superfine
(caster) sugar, plus extra
for sprinkling*

pinch of salt

1 tablespoon butter, melted

*1 lb (500 g) pitted dates,
coarsely chopped*

*2 oz (60 g) walnuts,
coarsely chopped*

6 oz (185 g) self-rising flour

1 tablespoon hot water

❖ Preheat an oven to 375°F (190°C/Gas Mark 5). Lightly butter a 7 x 11 x 1½-inch (18 x 28 x 4-cm) cake pan.

❖ Beat the eggs, sugar, salt, and butter until creamy. Mix in the dates and walnuts. Sift the flour, then fold it into the date mixture. Add the hot water and mix well.

❖ Spread the mixture into the prepared pan. Bake for 25 minutes. Allow to cool in the pan, then cut into fingers and sprinkle with a little sugar. The date sticks may be served plain or buttered.

icing for grown-ups

rum and ginger icing

1½ oz (45 g) chopped candied (glacé) ginger, plus extra for decoration (optional)

1 tablespoon rum

½ cup (3½ oz/105 g) brown sugar

½ cup (4 fl oz/125 ml) heavy (double) cream

2 tablespoons (1 oz/30 g) butter

❖ Soak the ginger in the rum for 30 minutes. Combine the sugar and one-third of the cream in a saucepan. Bring to a boil over medium heat, then simmer for 10 minutes. Remove from heat and whisk in the butter, ginger, and rum. Refrigerate for 10 minutes, or until cool.

❖ Beat the remaining cream until soft peaks form. Gently fold into the cooled mixture. Use a palette knife or spatula to spread the icing evenly. Decorate with the extra chopped ginger, if desired.

makes about 1 cup (8 fl oz/250 ml)

orange liqueur icing

1 cup (8 oz/250 g) sweet (unsalted) butter

1 tablespoon orange juice

1 tablespoon Cointreau or Grand Marnier

2½ cups (10 oz/310 g) confectioners' (icing) sugar, sifted

❖ Using an electric mixer, beat the butter until light and fluffy. Stir in the orange juice and liqueur, then gradually beat in the sugar until smooth. Use a palette knife or spatula to spread the icing evenly.

makes about 2 cups (16 fl oz/500 ml)

apple and almond
squares

makes 16

The flavors of apples and almonds marry well. In this recipe, they are combined with dates, oats, and brown sugar to make wholesome, fruity bar cookies.

2 cups (6 oz/185 g) rolled oats

1½ cups (6 oz/185 g) self-rising flour

1 teaspoon baking powder

large pinch of salt

¾ cup (6 oz/185 g) butter or margarine

½ cup (3½ oz/105 g) packed brown sugar

⅓ cup (2 oz/60 g) slivered (flaked) almonds

1 large cooking apple, peeled, cored, and coarsely chopped

¾ cup (4 oz/125 g) pitted dates, chopped

2 large eggs

1 tablespoon milk

❖ Preheat an oven to 375°F (190°C/Gas Mark 5). Lightly grease an 8-inch (20-cm) square cake pan. Line the base and sides of the pan with parchment (baking) paper.

❖ In a bowl, mix together 5½ oz (170 g) of the oats, the flour, baking powder, and salt. With your fingertips, rub in the butter or margarine until the mixture resembles fine breadcrumbs. Mix in the sugar and 1½ oz (45 g) of the almonds. Add the apple and dates.

❖ Beat together the eggs and milk. Add to the flour mixture and mix well.

❖ Spread the mixture into the prepared pan. Smooth the surface with a palette knife. Sprinkle over the remaining ½ oz (15 g) oats and ½ oz (15 g) almonds.

❖ Bake until golden and cooked, about 45 minutes. Cool in the pan, then cut into 2-inch (5-cm) squares.

recipe variation

Raisins or golden raisins (sultanas) may replace the dates in this recipe.

cherry cookies

makes about 30

These cookies are quick and
easy to make and will
always be a welcome
addition to the cookie jar.

½ cup (4 oz/125 g) butter or margarine

½ cup (4 oz/125 g) superfine (caster) sugar

1 egg, separated

½ cup chopped maraschino (glacé) cherries

2 cups (8 oz/250 g) all-purpose (plain) flour

❖ Preheat an oven to 350°F (180°C/Gas Mark 4). Lightly butter baking sheets or line them with parchment (baking) paper.

❖ Cream together the butter and sugar using an electric mixer on medium to high speed until light and fluffy. Add the egg yolk and beat well. Stir in the cherries and the sifted flour. Knead lightly, then wrap in plastic wrap and chill for 30 minutes.

❖ Turn out onto a work surface and roll out between 2 sheets of parchment (baking) paper to a thickness of ¼ inch (6 mm). Using a 2-inch (5-cm) plain or fluted cookie cutter, cut out rounds. Place on the prepared baking sheets. Bake for 10–12 minutes or until light golden. Let cool for a few minutes on the baking sheets then transfer to wire racks to cool completely.

recipe variation

Replace the candied cherries with the same amount of candied (glacé) ginger, apricots, or pineapple.

banana
oaties

makes about 30

Packed with banana and oats, these cookies make a healthful and delicious snack. If you prefer a spicier cookie, increase the amount of cinnamon and nutmeg.

¾ cup (6 oz/185 g) butter or margarine

1 cup (7 oz/220 g) firmly packed brown sugar

1 egg, beaten

1½ cups (6 oz/185 g) whole-grain (wholemeal) flour

1 teaspoon baking soda (bicarbonate of soda)

½ teaspoon salt

1 teaspoon ground cinnamon

½ teaspoon ground nutmeg

1 cup (8 oz/250 g) mashed banana

1 cup (6 oz/185 g) steel-cut oats or oatmeal

❖ Preheat an oven to 400°F (200°C/Gas Mark 5). Lightly butter baking sheets or line them with parchment (baking) paper.

❖ Cream the butter or margarine and sugar using an electric mixer on medium to high speed until light and fluffy. Add the egg and beat well.

❖ Sift together the flour, baking soda, salt, cinnamon, and nutmeg. Add to the butter and sugar mixture along with the banana and oatmeal. Mix until all ingredients are thoroughly combined.

❖ Drop heaping tablespoons of the mixture onto the prepared baking sheets. Bake for 12–15 minutes or until lightly browned. Transfer to wire racks to cool.

oatmeal and golden raisin cookies

makes about 30

For a change, make this recipe with the same weight of chopped dried apples, chopped dried apricots, or chopped raisins.

1/2 cup (4 oz/125 g) butter or margarine

1/2 cup (4 oz/125 g) raw sugar

1 egg

1 tablespoon orange juice

3 tablespoons milk

1 cup (6 oz/185 g) steel-cut oats or oatmeal

1 1/4 cups (5 oz/155 g) whole-grain (wholemeal) self-rising flour

1 teaspoon ground cinnamon

pinch of salt

1 cup (6 oz/185 g) golden raisins (sultanas)

❖ Preheat an oven to 350°F (180°C/Gas Mark 4). Lightly butter baking sheets or line them with parchment (baking) paper.

❖ Cream the butter or margarine and sugar using an electric mixer on medium to high speed until light and fluffy. Add the egg, orange juice, and milk; beat well.

❖ Mix together the oats or oatmeal, sifted flour, cinnamon, and salt. Add to the butter and sugar mixture along with the golden raisins. Mix until all ingredients are thoroughly combined.

❖ Drop heaping tablespoons of the mixture onto the prepared baking sheets. Bake for 12–15 minutes or until lightly browned. Transfer to wire racks to cool.

coconut
cookies

coconut puffs

makes about 20

1 egg, lightly beaten

¼ cup (2 fl oz/60 ml) milk

1 teaspoon vanilla extract (essence)

1 cup (7 oz/220 g) superfine (caster) sugar

2½ cups (7½ oz/235 g) grated dried (desiccated) coconut

2 tablespoons self-rising flour

❖ Preheat an oven to 325°F (160°C/Gas Mark 3). Grease a baking sheet with vegetable oil or line it with parchment (baking) paper.

❖ Combine the beaten egg, milk, and vanilla in a jug. Place the sugar, coconut, and flour in a bowl. Add the egg mixture and mix until well combined. Place heaping teaspoons of the mixture on the prepared baking sheet. Bake for 20 minutes, or until golden. Transfer to wire racks to cool.

coconut
macadamia
cookies

makes about 70

Although pecans or almonds are delicious additions to these cookies, there really is no substitute for the mild, buttery taste of macadamia nuts. They usually cost a little more, but we think they're worth it.

½ cup (4 oz/125 g) butter or margarine, softened

1 cup (8 oz/250 g) granulated (white) sugar

½ teaspoon baking soda (bicarbonate of soda)

2 eggs

½ cup (4 fl oz/125 ml) sour cream

1 teaspoon vanilla extract (essence)

2½ cups (10 oz/315 g) all-purpose (plain) flour

2 cups (6 oz/240 g) grated dried (desiccated) coconut

1½ cups (8 oz/250 g) chopped macadamia nuts, pecans, or almonds

❖ Preheat an oven to 350°F (180°C/Gas Mark 4). In a mixing bowl beat the butter or margarine with an electric mixer on medium to high speed for 30 seconds. Add the sugar and baking soda and beat until combined. Beat in the eggs, sour cream, and vanilla. Beat in as much of the flour as you can with the mixer. Stir in any remaining flour with a wooden spoon. Stir in the coconut and nuts.

❖ Drop rounded teaspoons of the dough onto ungreased baking sheets, spacing them 2 inches (5 cm) apart. Bake for 10–12 minutes, or until golden brown. Transfer to wire racks to cool.

recipe hint

It is easiest to use 2 teaspoons to drop the cookie dough onto the baking sheets. Scoop up the dough with 1 teaspoon, then use the back of the other to push it onto the baking sheet. For uniform results, try using a small, spring-loaded ice-cream scoop to shape and drop the cookie dough.

muesli-apricot squares with yogurt topping

makes 16

Drying fruit intensifies its natural flavor and concentrates its sweetness. The chopped dried apricots in these squares give a burst of fruity flavor. You could try using dried dates, figs, or pears instead, if you like.

1 cup (6 oz/185 g) untoasted (natural) muesli

1 cup (4 oz/125 g) self-rising flour, sifted

1½ cups (4½ oz/140 g) rolled oats

⅔ cup (2 oz/60 g) grated dried (desiccated) coconut

1 cup (4 oz/125 g) finely chopped dried apricots

½ cup (3 oz/90 g) lightly packed dark brown sugar

¾ cup (6 oz/185 g) butter

2 tablespoons cornsyrup, light molasses, or golden syrup

1 large egg, lightly beaten

YOGURT TOPPING

2 tablespoons plain yogurt

❖ Preheat an oven to 350°F (180°C/Gas Mark 4). Lightly grease a 10-inch (25-cm) square cake pan or line it with parchment (baking) paper.

❖ In a large bowl combine the muesli, flour, oats, and coconut. Stir in the apricots and brown sugar. In a small pan over low heat, melt together the butter and cornsyrup, light molasses, or golden syrup. Pour the butter mixture over the dry ingredients, add the lightly beaten egg, and mix well. Press firmly into the prepared pan. Bake for 25–30 minutes, or until firm to the touch and lightly golden. Allow to cool in the pan.

❖ For the topping, beat together the yogurt and confectioners' sugar until smooth. Spread evenly over the cooked base and cut into squares.

storage hint

These squares will keep, unfrosted, for over a week in an airtight container.

choc-coconut
brownies

makes about 18

The dried flesh of the coconut adds an exotic taste and texture to many baked treats, and these moreish brownies are no exception. Store dried coconut in an airtight container and it will keep for months.

$2/3$ cup (5 oz/155 g) butter, softened

1 cup (5 oz/155 g) lightly packed brown sugar

3 eggs

$2/3$ cup ($2^1/2$ oz/75 g) unsweetened cocoa powder

1 cup (4 oz/125 g) self-rising flour

1 cup (3 oz/90 g) flaked dried coconut

$2/3$ cup (1 oz/30 g) grated dried (desiccated) coconut

CHOCOLATE FROSTING

2 tablespoons sweet (unsalted) butter, softened

3 tablespoons unsweetened cocoa powder

$1^1/2$ cups (8 oz/250 g) confectioners' (icing) sugar, sifted

milk, as needed

✤ Preheat an oven to 350°F (180°C/Gas Mark 4).
Line an 8-inch (20-cm) square cake pan with parchment
(baking) or waxed (greaseproof) paper and then
butter the paper.

✤ In a bowl, cream the butter and brown sugar,
then beat in the eggs, one at a time. Sift the cocoa and
flour together into the bowl, then add the coconut and
stir until well combined. Spread the mixture firmly and
evenly into the prepared pan and bake for about
35–40 minutes. It will still feel soft while hot but will
firm up as it cools. Allow to cool in the pan. When
completely cool, turn onto a wire rack and frost.

✤ For the frosting, cream the butter and cocoa,
then stir in the sifted confectioners' sugar. Gradually
stir in enough milk to make a thick frosting. Spread
evenly over the brownies and cut into squares.

recipe hint

Use a rubber spatula to
transfer the brownie mixture
to the prepared pan.
Spread it evenly and firmly
into the pan, making sure
that each corner of the
pan is completely filled.

coconut orange wafers

makes about 60

Two tropical flavors combine to add both taste and texture to these crisp wafers. Serve them with ice cream, if you like.

1/2 cup (4 oz/125 g) butter or margarine, softened

1/3 cup (3 oz/90 g) cream cheese, softened

1 1/2 cups (6 oz/185 g) sifted confectioners' (icing) sugar

1/4 teaspoon baking soda (bicarbonate of soda)

1/4 teaspoon salt

1 egg

1 tablespoon milk

1 teaspoon finely shredded orange zest (rind)

1/4 teaspoon coconut extract (essence)

2 1/2 cups (10 oz/315 g) all-purpose (plain) flour

1/2–3/4 cup (1 1/2–2 1/2 oz/45–75 g) grated dried (desiccated) coconut, lightly toasted

❖ In a large mixing bowl beat the butter or margarine and cream cheese with an electric mixer on medium to high speed for 30 seconds. Add the confectioners' sugar, baking soda, and salt; beat until combined. Beat in the egg, milk, orange zest, and coconut extract. Beat in as much of the flour as you can with the mixer. Stir in any remaining flour with a wooden spoon.

❖ Divide the dough in half. If necessary, cover and chill for 1 hour, or until the dough can be shaped into rolls. Shape each portion into an 8-inch (20-cm) roll. Roll in the toasted coconut to coat completely. Wrap each roll in waxed (greaseproof) paper or plastic wrap. Chill for 2 hours, or until firm.

❖ Preheat an oven to 375°F (190°C/Gas Mark 4). Cut the dough into ¼-inch (6-mm) thick slices. Place on ungreased baking sheets, spacing them 2 inches (5 cm) apart. Bake for 7–9 minutes, or until lightly browned. Transfer the wafers to a rack to cool.

recipe variations

Try using lemon or lime zest instead of the orange zest in this recipe for a different citrus flavor. When peeling the zest, be sure to use only the thin, colored top layer and not the bitter white pith underneath.

coconut and almond
macaroons

makes 20–25

Toasted almonds give these macaroons a delicious nutty flavor, while the addition of lemon zest provides a tangy citrus note. They're the perfect accompaniment to a hot cup of tea or coffee.

4 egg whites, at room temperature

1/4 teaspoon salt

1 teaspoon fresh lemon juice

1 cup (8 oz/250 g) superfine (caster) sugar

1/2 teaspoon ground cinnamon

1/2 cup (1 1/2 oz/45 g) grated dried (desiccated) coconut

1 cup (3 1/2 oz/100 g) toasted and ground almonds

1/2 cup (3 oz/90 g) arrowroot

1 teaspoon grated lemon zest (rind)

1 teaspoon vanilla extract (essence)

❖ Preheat an oven to 375°F (190°C/Gas Mark 4). Line a baking sheet with parchment (baking) or waxed (greaseproof) paper and then lightly grease the paper.

❖ Using an electric mixer, beat the egg whites with the salt until stiff peaks form (tips stand straight when the beaters are lifted out of the mixture). Combine the lemon juice and sugar and gradually beat into the egg whites. Fold in the combined cinnamon, coconut, almonds, and arrowroot, the lemon zest, and vanilla.

❖ Drop teaspoons of the mixture onto the prepared baking sheet, spacing them about ¾ inch (2 cm) apart. Bake for 10–15 minutes, or until light golden in color and almost firm to the touch. Transfer to a wire rack and allow to cool completely before serving.

recipe hint

Egg whites are usually beaten until either soft or stiff peaks form. The soft peak stage is reached when the egg whites are foamy and the tips of the peaks bend over when the beaters are lifted out.
The stiff peak stage is reached when the egg whites are glossy and form stiff peaks that hold their shape when the beaters are lifted out.

nut *cookies*

hazelnut toffee bars

makes about 36

These toffee confections are like melt-in-the-mouth homemade candies. Sprinkle broken toffee or crushed nut brittle (recipes page 212) over the top instead of nuts for a decadent touch.

1 cup (8 oz/250 g) butter or margarine, softened

1/2 cup (31/2 oz/105 g) packed brown sugar

1/2 teaspoon salt

3 tablespoons milk

1 teaspoon vanilla extract (essence)

2 cups (8 oz/250 g) all-purpose (plain) flour

1 cup (4 oz/125 g) finely chopped hazelnuts (filberts), pecans, or walnuts

9 oz (280 g) good-quality sweet (milk) chocolate bars, each 11/2 oz (45 g)

hazelnut toffee bars

❖ Preheat an oven to 350°F (180°C/Gas Mark 4). Grease a 13 x 9 x 2-inch (33 x 23 x 5-cm) baking pan and then line it with parchment (baking) paper. In a medium mixing bowl beat the butter or margarine with an electric mixer on medium to high speed for 30 seconds. Add the brown sugar and salt and beat until combined. Beat in the milk and vanilla. Beat in as much of the flour as you can with the mixer. Stir in any remaining flour with a wooden spoon. Stir in half of the hazelnuts, pecans, or walnuts.

❖ Spread batter in prepared pan. Bake for 20–25 minutes, or until lightly browned around the edges.

❖ Immediately place the chocolate bars on top of the hot crust. Set aside for 2–3 minutes, or until the chocolate melts. Spread the chocolate evenly over the crust, then sprinkle with the remaining nuts. Cool in the pan on a wire rack. Cut into bars.

recipe hint

Miniature chocolate bars make a quick, easy icing in this recipe. Arrange the unwrapped chocolate bars in 2 even rows over the hot crust. Once they have melted, simply spread them over the crust using an icing knife or small spatula. Make some swirls and ridges for texture, if you like.

mexican peanut cookies

2½ cups (10 oz/315 g) all-purpose (plain) flour

1 teaspoon baking powder

3½ oz (105 g) lard, chopped

1 egg

3½ oz (105 g) peanuts, shelled, skinned, toasted, and ground to a paste in a food processor

⅔ cup (5 oz/155 g) sugar

makes about 40

These cookies come from the Veracruz region, where peanuts are grown locally. They can be served for breakfast or as a mid-morning snack with coffee or hot chocolate.

Mexican peanut cookies

❖ Preheat an oven to 300°F (150°C/Gas Mark 2).
Lightly butter baking sheets.

❖ Sift the flour with the baking powder onto a work
surface. Make a well in the center and add the lard and
egg. Combine the ingredients with your fingers to
make a smooth dough. Add the peanut paste and
knead the dough lightly.

❖ Roll the dough into walnut-sized balls and place on
the prepared baking sheets, spacing them 3 inches
(7.5 cm) apart. Flatten the balls slightly. Bake for
20–25 minutes, or until they turn a light golden brown.

❖ Remove the cookies from the oven and sprinkle
generously with sugar while they are still warm.

recipe hint

Although they are usually
referred to as nuts, peanuts
are actually legumes. They are
very nutritious, being high in
protein, fat, and dietary fibre,
and are a good source of
vitamin E and other vitamins.

almond cookies

makes 18

Almonds are one of the most popular nuts used in cooking, and feature in both savory and sweet recipes, such as these delicious cookies. Amaretto is a liqueur made from bitter almonds, apricot kernels, and aromatic extracts.

1/2 cup plus 2 tablespoons (3 oz/100 g) blanched almonds

1/4 cup (1 3/4 oz/55 g) superfine (caster) sugar

1 small egg, beaten

1/2 teaspoon amaretto or almond extract (essence)

1/4 cup (1 3/4 oz/55 g) superfine (caster) sugar, extra

almond cookies

❖ Preheat an oven to 350°F (180°C/Gas Mark 4). Line a baking sheet with parchment (baking) or waxed (greaseproof) paper.

❖ Combine almonds and sugar in a food processor and process to a fine meal. With the machine running, add enough of the beaten egg and amaretto or almond extract so the mixture just comes together.

❖ Transfer the mixture to a work surface and pat it together into a circle. Place the extra sugar in a small bowl. Divide the dough into 3 equal portions. Roll each portion into a 1-inch (2.5-cm) wide rope. Cut each rope into 6 even pieces. Roll each piece into a ball, then roll in the extra sugar to coat.

❖ Place on the prepared baking sheet, spacing the balls 1 inch (2.5 cm) apart. Bake for 15 minutes, until just pale. Transfer to a wire rack to cool. Serve alone or with Berries with Whipped Cream (right).

serving suggestion

This delicious recipe is a perfect accompaniment for almond cookies, and turns a plate of cookies into an instant dessert.

berries with whipped cream

1 cup (4 oz/125 g) mixed berries such as raspberries, blueberries, and strawberries

2 tablespoons confectioners' (icing) sugar, sifted

1/2 cup (4 fl oz/125 ml) heavy (double) cream, whipped

❖ Cut any larger berries in half. Fold the confectioners' sugar into the whipped cream. Gently fold in the berries. Serve immediately with the almond cookies.

using nuts

Chopped nuts make an ideal topping for all kinds of cookies, and are even tastier when they are toasted, which enhances their flavor and deepens their color.

toasting nuts

Preheat an oven to 350°F (180°C/Gas Mark 4). Spread the nuts in a single layer on a baking sheet. Bake until nuts are a light golden brown and are fragrant, 5–10 minutes. Stir occasionally with a wooden spoon to ensure the nuts brown evenly. Some, like pine nuts, burn easily, so check often.

skinning hazelnuts (filberts)

Roast nuts first (as above). When cool enough to handle, place in a kitchen towel, gather it into a bundle, and rub vigorously. (Don't worry about the skins that don't come off.) Allow to cool completely before using.

peeling almonds

Place in a heatproof bowl. Cover with boiling water and set aside for 5–10 minutes. Using a slotted spoon, remove a few almonds at a time. Squeeze the blunt end of the nut between your fingers; it should slip easily out of its skin. If not, return to the water for a few more minutes. Dry completely before using.

sifting nuts

Spoon roasted and chopped nuts into a fine sieve over paper towels. Tap the edge of the sieve to filter out the skins.

note: child safety

Coarsely chopped nuts on top of cookies can cause choking in very young children. Nonpareils or sprinkles are a safer option.

nut brittles

Butter brittle (or brickle) is golden-brown, buttery, hard pieces of toffee. The addition of nuts gives extra flavor and texture. You can add butter or nut brittle to cookie doughs and batters as directed in the recipe, scatter them over freshly baked cookies, or sprinkle them over ice cream for dessert. Butter brittle is available in the confectionery section of most supermarkets, but making your own delicious nut brittle is quick and easy. Place it in a heavy-duty plastic bag and use a rolling pin to crush for finer pieces.

almond brittle

2 tablespoons sweet almond oil

2½ cups (20 oz/625 g) sugar

few drops of fresh lemon juice

3 cups (16 oz/500 g) raw almonds, peeled (see page 211 for how to peel almonds)

❖ Use the sweet almond oil to grease a marble slab and a rolling pin.

❖ Heat the sugar and lemon juice over medium heat in a (preferably) copper saucepan or any heavy pan. Stir gently with a spatula to ensure the sugar dissolves thoroughly and doesn't stick to the sides of the pan.

❖ When the sugar has completely dissolved, add the almonds and stir constantly until the mixture is golden. Pour the contents of the pan onto the greased marble slab. Using the greased rolling pin, quickly roll out to a thickness of ½ inch (12 mm). Allow to partially cool, then cut into 1½ x 4-inch (4 x 10-cm) strips. Allow to cool completely before serving.

makes about 24 pieces

microwave date and peanut brittle

1 cup (8 oz/250 g) sugar

½ cup (6 oz/185 g) honey

1 cup (5 oz/155 g) raw peanuts

½ cup (3 oz/90 g) roughly chopped, pitted dried dates

1 tablespoon butter

1 teaspoon baking powder

❖ Lightly grease an 8 x 12-inch (20 x 30-cm) baking pan or baking sheet.

❖ Place the sugar and honey in a 3–4 qt (3–4 l) microwave-safe dish or casserole. Cook on medium (50%) for 6–8 minutes, stirring well after 4 minutes. On removal, ensure that the sugar is completely dissolved. If not, cook for a little longer.

❖ Stir in the nuts and dates. Cook on high (100%) for 4–5 minutes, until the syrup is a rich golden color. Do not overcook. Stir in the butter and then the baking powder. As soon as the mixture begins to foam and appears creamy, quickly pour it into the prepared pan or baking sheet. Allow to cool, then break into pieces.

makes about 1 lb (500 g)

microwave pecan brittle

½ cup (4 oz/125 g) sugar

¼ cup (2 fl oz/60 ml) water

¾ cup (3 oz/90 g) pecans, chopped

❖ Lightly butter a baking sheet.

❖ Combine the sugar and water in a microwave-safe bowl and cook on high (100%) for 2 minutes. Stir until the sugar dissolves completely.

❖ Cook on high for a further 6–8 minutes, or until the mixture is golden brown. Immediately stir in the pecans. Pour the mixture onto the baking sheet, separating the nuts with a fork. Allow to cool and then coarsely chop.

makes about ½ lb (250 g)

glazed almond strips

makes about 50

As an alternative to making several 2½-inch (6-cm) strips with the cookie press, you can make 1 long strip and then cut it into the correct lengths with a knife.

¾ cup (6 oz/185 g) butter or margarine, softened

½ cup (3½ oz/105 g) packed brown sugar

2 teaspoons milk

few drops of almond extract (essence)

1¾ cups (7 oz/220 g) all-purpose (plain) flour

1 egg white, lightly beaten

½ cup (2 oz/60 g) sliced (flaked) almonds or pine nuts

1 teaspoon granulated (white) sugar

❖ Preheat an oven to 375°F (190°C/Gas Mark 4). In a mixing bowl beat the butter or margarine with an electric mixer on medium to high speed for 30 seconds. Add the brown sugar, milk, and almond extract; beat until combined. Mix in as much of the flour as you can with the mixer. Stir in any remaining flour with a wooden spoon. Do not chill the dough.

❖ Pack the dough into a cookie press fitted with a ribbon plate. Force the dough through the cookie press onto ungreased baking sheets, making 2½-inch (6-cm) ribbons, about 1 inch (2.5 cm) apart. Using a pastry brush, brush each cookie with egg white. Decorate the cookies with almonds or pine nuts, then sprinkle with granulated sugar.

❖ Bake for 7–8 minutes, or until edges are firm but not brown. Allow to cool for 1 minute on the baking sheets, then transfer to a wire rack to cool completely.

recipe hint

To make pressed cookie ribbons, hold the cookie press at an angle. Draw the press along the baking sheets in a straight line as you force out the dough. Lift up the cookie press when the cookie is the desired length.

peanut brittle
florentines

makes 12

As they bake, the heaping teaspoonfuls of caramel-colored batter spread into large, lacy cookies that become crisp and shiny when cooled. Spread them with melted chocolate and they are simply irresistible.

3 tablespoons sweet (unsalted) butter

2 tablespoons honey

1/4 cup (2 oz/60 g) packed brown sugar

1/4 cup (1 oz/30 g) all-purpose (plain) flour, sifted

1/4 cup (1 1/2 oz/45 g) raw peanuts, chopped

1/4 cup (1 oz/30 g) maraschino (glacé) cherries, chopped

3 1/2 oz (105 g) semisweet (plain) chocolate, melted

❖ Preheat an oven to 350°F (180°C/Gas Mark 4). Line 2 baking sheets with parchment (baking) or waxed (greaseproof) paper.

❖ Place the butter, honey, and brown sugar in a saucepan and bring to a boil over medium heat. Remove from the heat and allow to cool. Stir in the flour, peanuts, and cherries.

❖ Drop heaping teaspoons of the mixture onto the prepared baking sheets, spacing them 2 inches (5 cm) apart. Bake for 12–15 minutes, or until golden. Remove from the oven and allow to cool for 5 minutes on the baking sheets. Using a spatula, carefully transfer the florentines to a wire rack to cool completely.

❖ When completely cool, spread the smoothest side of each florentine with the melted chocolate. When the chocolate is almost set, make a wavy pattern using the tines of a fork. Allow to set completely before serving.

recipe variations

Candied (glacé) fruit is made by preserving whole, zest (rind), or pieces of fruit in a heavy sugar syrup. Other fruits that are commonly candied are citrus, pineapple, and apricots. Any of these can be used instead of the cherries, if desired.

The peanuts can also be replaced with other nuts, such as almonds, pecans, hazelnuts (filberts), or walnuts, if desired.

almond crisps

makes about 30

**Roll these cookies around
a spoon handle to make
tubular pirouettes or shape
them around inverted muffin
pans to create tulip cups. Dip
the pirouettes in melted
chocolate, if desired.
Fill the cups with custard,
chocolate mousse, whipped
cream, or ice cream and
fresh berries.**

¼ cup (2 oz/60 g) butter or margarine

2 egg whites, at room temperature

½ cup (4 oz/125 g) granulated (white) sugar

½ cup (2 oz/60 g) all-purpose (plain) flour

½ teaspoon almond extract (essence)

½ cup (2½ oz/75 g) semisweet (plain) chocolate,
chopped (optional)

2 teaspoons solid vegetable shortening
or butter (optional)

❖ Preheat an oven to 375°F (190°C/Gas Mark 4). Generously butter a baking sheet. (The baking sheet will need to re-buttered for each batch.) Set aside. In a small saucepan melt the butter or margarine over low heat. Set aside to cool.

❖ Beat the egg whites with an electric mixer on medium to high speed until soft peaks form (tips curl). Gradually add sugar, beating until stiff peaks form (tips stand straight). Fold in about half of the flour, then gently stir in melted butter or margarine and almond extract. Fold in the remaining flour until combined. Drop 3 level tablespoons of batter separately onto the prepared baking sheet, at least 3 inches (7.5 cm) apart, and spread each into a 3-inch (7.5-cm) circle. (Only 3 cookies are baked at a time.) Bake for 5–6 minutes, or until golden.

❖ Working quickly, remove a cookie from the baking sheet. To make a pirouette, place the cookie upside down on a work surface and quickly roll it around the greased handle of a wooden spoon or dowel. Or, to make a tulip cup, shape the warm cookie around an inverted muffin pan. Remove the cookie from the handle, dowel, or muffin pan and cool on a wire rack. Repeat with the remaining warm cookies. (If they harden before you can shape them, reheat them in the oven for about 1 minute.)

❖ To dip pirouettes, in a small, heavy saucepan heat chocolate and shortening or butter over low heat until just melted, stirring occasionally. Remove from heat. Dip 1 end of each pirouette in the chocolate mixture and let the excess drip off. (Or, drizzle cookies with chocolate mixture.) Transfer to a baking sheet lined with waxed (greaseproof) paper. Allow to set before serving.

pine nut cookies

makes 36

Not actually a nut at all, the pine nut is the edible seed from the cones of several varieties of pine trees. Softer and oilier than most nuts, they are at their best when lightly toasted. Watch them carefully when toasting, as they burn easily.

1 cup (4 oz/125 g) pine nuts

1½ cups (6 oz/185 g) all-purpose (plain) flour

¾ cup (4 oz/125 g) confectioners' (icing) sugar

½ teaspoon ground cinnamon

½ cup (4 oz/125 g) chilled sweet (unsalted) butter, chopped

1 teaspoon grated lemon zest (rind)

1 egg yolk

2 oz (60 g) semisweet (plain) chocolate, chopped

❖ Preheat an oven to 375°F (190°C/Gas Mark 4).

❖ Spread pine nuts on a baking sheet and toast in the oven until golden, about 5 minutes. Or, microwave on high (100%) for 2–3 minutes, stirring every minute. Cool, then grind finely in a food processor or blender.

❖ In a bowl, sift together the flour, sugar, and cinnamon. Rub in the butter with your fingers until the mixture resembles fine crumbs, then stir in the nuts, lemon zest, and egg yolk. Mix well. Add a little cold water to bring the dough together, if needed. Knead lightly, then roll out on a lightly floured board or between 2 sheets of parchment (baking) paper until ⅛ inch (3 mm) thick. Use a fluted 2-inch (5-cm) cutter to cut into rounds.

❖ Transfer to greased baking sheets and bake for 10–15 minutes, until golden. Transfer to a rack to cool.

❖ Melt the chocolate in the top half of a double boiler over simmering water. Dip 1 side of each cookie in the chocolate and refrigerate until set.

recipe variations

Toasted skinned hazelnuts can be used instead of pine nuts. If preferred, omit the chocolate and press coarsely chopped nuts on top of the cookies before baking.

peanut butter
bonbons

makes about 50

These are called bonbons because they have the look and richness of melt-in-the-mouth candies. They are easy to make.

1/2 cup (4 oz/125 g) butter or margarine, softened

1/2 cup (4 oz/125 g) crunchy peanut butter

3/4 cup (6 oz/185 g) packed brown sugar

1/4 teaspoon baking soda (bicarbonate of soda)

1 egg

1 1/2 teaspoons vanilla extract (essence)

2 1/2 cups (10 oz/315 g) all-purpose (plain) flour

2 cups (12 oz/375 g) semisweet (plain) chocolate, chopped

2 teaspoons solid vegetable shortening or butter

❖ Preheat an oven to 350°F (180°C/Gas Mark 4). In a large mixing bowl beat the butter or margarine and peanut butter with an electric mixer on medium to high speed for 30 seconds. Add the brown sugar and baking soda; beat until combined. Beat in the egg and vanilla. Beat in as much of the flour as you can with the mixer. Stir in any remaining flour with a wooden spoon.

❖ Shape the dough into 1-inch (2.5-cm) balls. Place on ungreased baking sheets, 1½ inches (4 cm) apart.

❖ Bake for 8–10 minutes, or until the cookies are set and lightly browned underneath. Transfer the cookies to a wire rack to cool.

❖ In a medium, heavy saucepan heat the chocolate and shortening over low heat until melted. Allow to cool slightly. Using a fork, dip the peanut butter balls, one at a time, in the chocolate mixture to coat. Transfer to baking sheets lined with waxed (greaseproof) paper and refrigerate until the bonbons are firm. Store in an airtight container in a cool place.

recipe hint

If the balls of dough are roughly the same size, they will bake in the same amount of time. Roll each portion of dough between the palms of your hands until nicely rounded and smooth all over.

almond cherry microwave cookies

makes about 24 cookies

These simple-to-make, old-fashioned cookies never go out of favor. Cooking them in the microwave takes very little time, so they're perfect to make for hungry kids.

½ cup (4 oz/125 g) peanut butter

3 tablespoons butter or margarine, softened

¾ cup (5½ oz/170 g) raw sugar

1 egg

½ teaspoon almond extract (essence)

1½ cups (6 oz/185 g) all-purpose (plain) flour

½ teaspoon baking powder

6 maraschino (glacé) cherries, halved

12 blanched almonds

❖ Place the peanut butter and butter or margarine in a large mixing bowl. Add the sugar and use electric beaters to cream the mixture until light and fluffy. Stir in the egg and almond extract. Sift together the flour and baking powder, then stir into the butter mixture to form a stiff dough.

❖ Roll teaspoons of the mixture into small balls.

❖ Cover a microwave-safe baking sheet or large plate with parchment (baking) paper. Place 6 balls, spaced well apart, on the plate. Flatten each lightly with the heel of your hand and place half a maraschino cherry or a blanched almond in the center of each.

❖ Cook on high (100%) for 1½–2 minutes, until cooked through and set. Allow to stand for 1–2 minutes to crisp a little before transferring to a wire rack to cool completely.

❖ Repeat with the remaining balls of cookie dough.

recipe variations

You can replace the cherries and almonds with different types of nuts, if desired. Try using peanuts, walnuts, or hazelnuts (filberts).

almond tuiles

makes about 12

"Tuile" is a French word that actually translates to "roof tile." In cooking, however, it is the name of a delicate, almond-flavored biscuit that is curled over a rolling pin immediately after being removed from the oven.

2 egg whites, at room temperature

1/2 cup (2 oz/60 g) confectioners' (icing) sugar, sifted

1/3 cup (1 1/3 oz/40 g) all-purpose (plain) flour, sifted

2 oz (60 g) butter, melted and cooled

4 oz (125 g) sliced (flaked) almonds

❖ Preheat an oven to 325°F (160°C/Gas Mark 3). Lightly butter 2 large nonstick baking sheets.

❖ Use electric beaters to beat the egg whites until soft peaks form (tips curl). Add the confectioners' sugar gradually, beating until smooth and glossy. Fold in the sifted flour. Pour the melted butter down the side of the bowl and use a metal spoon to gently fold in until combined.

❖ This quantity of dough will make either 12 medium or 6 large cookies. Depending on your choice, spoon 6 or 12 very thin circles of batter over the baking sheets. Use the back of a spoon to smooth the batter out as thinly as possible. Sprinkle the cookies evenly with the almonds.

❖ Slide 1 baking sheet into the oven and bake for 5–6 minutes. Watch carefully, as the tuiles must be golden but not burnt. Remove from the oven and, using a slotted spatula, immediately lift the cookies off the baking sheets. They will be soft and pliable. Arrange the cookies over the curve of a rolling pin if they are medium, or over a bottle if they are large. They will soon cool and hold their shape. When dry and firm, transfer to a wire rack to cool completely.

❖ Meanwhile, cook and shape the remaining tuiles the same way. Eat the tuiles soon after they are cooked.

recipe variations

Add candied (glacé) orange peel or tiny chocolate flakes (made by finely grating chocolate) to almond mixture, or replace almonds with thin strips of pistachios.

pecan florentines

makes about 36

These lacy cookies are buttery and crisp. Don't bake more than 5 cookies on the baking sheet at once because even a small amount of cookie batter will spread a lot.

¼ cup (2 oz/60 g) granulated (white) sugar

¼ cup (2 oz/60 g) butter or margarine, melted

1 tablespoon cornsyrup, light molasses, or golden syrup

1 tablespoon milk

¼ cup (1 oz/30 g) ground pecans or walnuts

¼ cup (1 oz/30 g) all-purpose (plain) flour, sifted

2 oz (60 g) sweet (milk) cooking chocolate or white chocolate, chopped

❖ Preheat an oven to 350°F (180°C/Gas Mark 4).
Line baking sheets with foil, then grease the foil.

❖ In a medium mixing bowl stir together the sugar,
melted butter or margarine, cornsyrup, and milk.
Stir in the ground pecans or walnuts and flour
until well combined.

❖ Drop level teaspoons of batter onto prepared baking
sheet, spacing them 5 inches (13 cm) apart. (Bake only
3–5 cookies at a time.) Bake for 5–6 minutes, or until
bubbly and deep golden brown. Cool cookies on the
baking sheet for 1–2 minutes, or until set. Quickly
transfer to a wire rack to cool. Repeat with the
remaining cookie batter.

❖ In a small, heavy saucepan melt the chocolate over
low heat. Drizzle over the cooled cookies.

recipe hint

To drizzle cookies with
chocolate, place on a wire
rack over waxed (greaseproof)
paper. Fill a teaspoon with
melted chocolate and move
back and forth over the
cookies to make fine lines.
Let the chocolate flow in a
thin stream. Or, spoon the
chocolate into a heavy-duty
plastic bag and cut a tiny
piece off one corner. Squeeze
the bag gently to pipe the
chocolate in a thin drizzle.

chocolate hazelnut
biscotti

makes about 35

1 cup (7 oz/220 g) superfine (caster) sugar

3 eggs

2 cups (8 oz/250 g) all-purpose (plain) flour

½ cup (2 oz/60 g) self-rising flour

½ cup (1½ oz/45 g) unsweetened cocoa powder

1 teaspoon baking soda (bicarbonate of soda)

¼ teaspoon salt

2 oz (60 g) chopped semisweet (plain) chocolate

½ cup (2½ oz/75 g) roughly chopped roasted hazelnuts (filberts)

❖ Preheat an oven to 325°F (160°C/ Gas Mark 3). Line a baking sheet with parchment (baking) paper.

❖ Use an electric mixer on medium speed to beat the sugar and eggs until pale and frothy, about 2 minutes. Use a large metal spoon to fold in the combined sifted flours, cocoa, baking soda, and salt. Fold in the chopped chocolate and the hazelnuts. Mix to a soft dough.

❖ Divide the dough in half. Briefly knead each portion on a lightly floured surface until smooth. Form each portion into a log 8 x 1½ inches (20 x 4 cm) thick. Place logs on prepared baking sheet, 4 inches (10 cm) apart. Bake for 45 minutes. Remove from the oven and allow to cool for 5 minutes.

❖ Using a serrated knife, cut each log into ½-inch (12-mm) slices, slightly on the diagonal. Return the slices to the baking tray. (You will need to bake in batches.) Bake for a further 15 minutes, turning the slices after about 7 minutes, until crisp and lightly golden.Transfer to a wire rack to cool and crisp further.

recipe hint

Biscotti means "twice cooked," which reflects the way in which these cookies are made. The mixture is first cooked as a loaf, which is then thinly sliced and baked again, producing crisp, porous cookies. Biscotti will keep in an airtight container for weeks. Should they become slightly stale, they can easily be revived by placing them in an oven preheated to 325°F (160°C/Gas Mark 3) for 5–7 minutes. With a spatula, transfer to a wire rack to cool and crisp.

Biscotti are traditionally served with Vin Santo, an Italian dessert wine into which they are dunked. Or, for a special treat, try dipping one end of each biscotti in melted semisweet (plain) chocolate. Allow to set before serving.

spiced biscotti

makes about 35

Biscotti are a traditional Italian treat often served with strong, hot coffee. The small, crisp slices are made for dunking.

1 cup (7 oz/220 g) superfine (caster) sugar

3 eggs

2½ cups (10 oz/315 g) all-purpose (plain) flour

½ cup (2 oz/60 g) self-rising flour

1 teaspoon baking soda (bicarbonate of soda)

½ teaspoon ground cinnamon

½ teaspoon ground nutmeg

½ teaspoon ground cloves

½ teaspoon salt

1½ teaspoons aniseed liqueur such as Pernod or Ouzo

1 cup (4½ oz/140 g) slivered almonds

❖ Preheat oven to 325°F (160°C/Gas Mark 3). Line a baking sheet with parchment (baking) paper.

❖ Use an electric mixer to beat the sugar and eggs until pale and frothy, about 2 minutes. Use a large metal spoon to fold in the combined sifted flours, baking soda, spices, and salt. Fold in the aniseed liqueur and slivered almonds. Mix to a soft dough.

❖ Divide the dough in half. Briefly knead each portion on a lightly floured surface until smooth. Form each portion into a log 8 x 1½-inches (20 x 4-cm) thick. Place the logs on the prepared sheet, spacing them 4 inches (10 cm) apart. Bake for 45 minutes. Remove from the oven and allow to cool for 5 minutes.

❖ Using a serrated knife, cut each log into ½-inch (12-mm) slices, slightly on the diagonal. Return the slices to the baking tray. (You will need to bake in batches.) Bake for a further 15 minutes, turning the slices after about 7 minutes, until crisp and lightly golden. Transfer to a wire rack to cool and crisp further.

recipe hint

Anise is a herb native to the Middle East, cultivated mainly for its strong, licorice-flavored seeds called aniseed. Aniseed can be used to flavor cookies, cakes, breads, salads, soups, vegetables, fish, and poultry.

polvorones

makes about 36

**Polvorone comes from the
Spanish word *polvo*,
meaning "dust." These
cookies are very popular in
both Spain and Mexico,
where they are known as
Mexican Wedding Cookies.**

½ cup (4 oz/125 g) butter, softened

½ cup (4 oz/125 g) lard, chopped

½ cup (4 oz/125 g) sugar

2 large egg yolks

1 large orange

2 cups (8 oz/250 g) all-purpose (plain) flour, sifted

2 cups (8 oz/250 g) almond meal
(finely ground almonds)

confectioners' (icing) sugar, for dusting (optional)

❖ Preheat an oven to 400°F (200°C/Gas Mark 5).
Lightly butter baking sheets.

❖ In a mixing bowl beat the butter, lard, and sugar
to a smooth, light cream. Add the egg yolks separately,
beating well after each addition. Very finely grate the
orange zest (rind), then juice the orange. Add the zest
and juice to the batter, then fold in the flour and
almond meal. The dough should be quite crumbly. Add
a little water if needed to bring the dough together.

❖ Turn the dough onto a floured work surface and roll
out until ¾ inch (2 cm) thick. Use a 1¼-inch (3-cm)
cookie cutter to cut out rounds of dough. Place on the
prepared baking sheets and bake for about 15 minutes,
until cooked but still golden. The cookies will still feel
soft but will firm as they cool. Before serving, dust with
confectioners' sugar, if desired.

recipe hint

These delicate cookies
crumble easily. Traditionally,
they are wrapped in tissue
paper with both ends
twisted to look like bonbons,
to protect them.

hazelnut
macaroons

makes 12–15

Also known as filberts, hazelnuts are small, round, pale brown nuts that are enclosed in a hard brown shell with a pointed tip. They are an excellent source of vitamin E and are high in monounsaturated fat.

1/2 cup (3 oz/90 g) whole hazelnuts (filberts)

1 cup (6 oz/185 g) confectioners' (icing) sugar, sifted, plus extra for dusting (optional)

1/4 teaspoon baking soda (bicarbonate of soda)

2 egg whites, at room temperature

❖ Preheat an oven to 350°F (180°C/Gas Mark 4).

❖ Spread the hazelnuts on a baking sheet and toast in the oven for 8 minutes, stirring occasionally with a wooden spoon to ensure they toast evenly. Remove from the oven and, when cool enough to handle, place in a kitchen towel and rub vigorously to remove the skins. (Not all of the skins will come off; don't worry about those that do not.) Allow to cool, then place in a food processor and process until finely ground.

❖ Sift together the confectioners' sugar and baking soda. Mix in the ground hazelnuts.

❖ Reduce the oven temperature to 250°F (120°C/Gas Mark 1). Line a baking sheet with parchment (baking) or waxed (greaseproof) paper.

❖ Beat the egg whites until stiff peaks form (tips stand straight). Fold in the hazelnut mixture.

❖ Using a pastry (piping) bag, pipe about twelve 3-inch (8-cm) rounds of mixture onto the prepared baking sheet. Bake for 5 minutes. Reduce the oven temperature to 225°F (110°C/Gas Mark ½) and bake for a further 30–35 minutes. Remove from the oven and set aside to cool on the baking sheet. Repeat with the remaining cookie mixture.

❖ Before serving, dust with sifted confectioners' sugar, if desired.

amaretti

makes about 40

**Perfect for a light ending
to a big meal, amaretti are
puffy confections served
frequently in Italy. A cup of
espresso or cappuccino
would complement
them perfectly.**

1¼ cups (7 oz/220 g) blanched almonds

¾ cup (6 oz/185 g) granulated (white) sugar

2 egg whites, at room temperature

¼ teaspoon cream of tartar

¼ teaspoon almond extract (essence)

½ cup (2 oz/60 g) sliced (flaked) almonds

❖ Preheat an oven to 300°F (150°C/Gas Mark 2). Line 2 baking sheets with parchment (baking) or waxed (greaseproof) paper. Use a food processor or blender to process or blend the whole almonds with ¼ cup (2 oz/60 g) of the sugar until the almonds are finely ground. Set aside.

❖ Place the egg whites, cream of tartar, and almond extract in a mixing bowl. Use an electric mixer on medium speed to beat until soft peaks form (tips curl when beaters are lifted out of the mixture). Gradually add the remaining sugar, 1 tablespoon at a time, beating on high speed until very stiff peaks form (tips stand straight when beaters are lifted out of the mixture) and the sugar is almost dissolved. Fold in the almond mixture with a metal spoon.

❖ Drop rounded teaspoonfuls of meringue mixture onto the prepared baking sheets, spacing them 1½ inches (4 cm) apart. Sprinkle each cookie with a few sliced almonds. Bake for 12–15 minutes, or until the cookies just begin to brown (the centers will still be soft). Turn off the oven and let the cookies dry in the oven with the door closed for 30 minutes. Peel the cookies from the paper. Store in an airtight container in a cool, dry place for up to 1 week.

makes about 25

1/2 cup (4 oz/125 g) butter or margarine, softened

1 cup (7 oz/220 g) packed brown sugar

2 teaspoons baking powder

1 egg

2 teaspoons vanilla extract (essence)

2 cups (8 oz/250 g) all-purpose (plain) flour

1 cup (4 oz/125 g) toasted chopped pecans or walnuts

1/2 cup (3 oz/90 g) semisweet (plain) chocolate chips

1 teaspoon solid vegetable shortening

❖ Preheat an oven to 375°F (190°C/Gas Mark 4).

❖ In a mixing bowl beat the butter or margarine with an electric mixer on medium to high speed for 30 seconds. Add the brown sugar and baking powder; beat until combined. Beat in the egg and vanilla, then as much of the flour as you can with the mixer. Stir in any remaining flour with a wooden spoon. Stir in the pecans or walnuts.

❖ Drop rounded teaspoons of dough onto ungreased baking sheets, spacing them 2 inches (5 cm) apart. Bake for 8–10 minutes, or until golden-brown underneath. Transfer to wire racks to cool.

❖ In a small, heavy-duty plastic bag, combine the chocolate chips and shortening. Close the bag just above the chocolate, then place in a bowl of warm water until the chocolate melts. Snip off 1/8 inch (3 mm) of the corner of the bag. Gently squeeze the bag to pipe the chocolate mixture over cookies. Or, melt the chocolate and shortening in a saucepan over low heat. Cool for 5 minutes, then drizzle over cookies with a spoon. Let the cookies stand until the chocolate is set.

chocolate-drizzled
praline
cookies

linzer
sandwich rings

makes about 36

⅔ cup (5 oz/155 g) butter or
margarine, softened

½ cup (3½ oz/105 g) packed brown sugar

1½ teaspoons baking powder

1 teaspoon finely shredded
lemon zest (rind)

1 teaspoon ground cinnamon

¼ teaspoon ground allspice

¼ teaspoon salt

2 egg yolks

1 teaspoon vanilla extract (essence)

2 cups (8 oz/250 g) all-purpose
(plain) flour

1 cup (4 oz/125 g) ground almonds
or walnuts

confectioners' (icing) sugar, for dusting

¼ cup (2 oz/60 g) seedless raspberry jam

❖ Preheat an oven to 375°F (190°C/Gas Mark 4).

❖ In a large mixing bowl beat the butter or margarine with an electric mixer on medium to high speed for 30 seconds. Add the brown sugar, baking powder, lemon zest, cinnamon, allspice, and salt; beat until combined. Beat in the egg yolks and vanilla. Beat in as much of the flour as you can with the mixer. Stir in any remaining flour and the ground almonds or walnuts with a wooden spoon. Divide the dough in half. Cover and chill for 1 hour, or until the dough is easy to handle.

❖ On a lightly floured surface, roll each half of dough until ⅛-inch (3-mm) thick. Use a 2–2½-inch (5–6-cm) star-shaped, heart-shaped, or scalloped round biscuit cutter to cut out dough. Place shapes 1 inch (2.5 cm) apart on ungreased baking sheets. Use a 1-inch (2.5-cm) cutter to cut out the centers of half the unbaked cookies. Remove the centers, reroll the dough, and repeat until all the dough is used.

❖ Bake for 7–9 minutes, or until the edges are firm and cookies are browned underneath. Use a spatula to transfer to a wire rack to cool.

❖ To assemble cookie sandwiches, sift confectioners' sugar over the tops of the cookies with cutout centers. Set aside. Spread ½ teaspoon of jam onto the bottom of each remaining cookie; top with a cutout cookie, sugar-side up. (Store cookies without confectioners' sugar and jam, then assemble up to several hours before serving.)

almond half-moons

makes about 70

1 cup (8 oz/250 g) butter
or margarine, softened

½ cup (4 oz/125 g)
granulated (white) sugar

1 egg

¼ teaspoon almond
extract (essence)

2¼ cups (9 oz/280 g)
all-purpose (plain) flour

¾ cup (3 oz/90 g) ground
almonds, hazelnuts
(filberts), or pecans

sifted confectioners'
(icing) sugar

❖ Preheat an oven to 375°F (190°C/Gas Mark 4).

❖ In a large mixing bowl beat the butter or margarine with an electric mixer on medium to high speed for 30 seconds. Add the sugar; beat until combined. Beat in the egg and almond extract. Beat in as much of the flour as you can with the mixer. Stir in any remaining flour and the ground nuts with a wooden spoon.

❖ Pack the dough into a cookie press fitted with a ½-inch (12-mm) wide round or star nozzle. Force dough through the press onto ungreased baking sheets to form crescent shapes, about 2½ inches (6 cm) long and 1 inch (2.5 cm) apart.

❖ Bake for 6–8 minutes, or until edges are firm and cookies are lightly browned underneath. Transfer to a wire rack to cool. Sprinkle cooled cookies with confectioners' sugar.

244

almond biscotti

makes 48

1 cup (7 oz/220 g)
superfine (caster) sugar

3 eggs

2 teaspoons finely shredded
lemon zest (rind)

1 teaspoon almond
extract (essence)

2½ cups (10 oz/315 g) all-purpose
(plain) flour

½ cup (2 oz/60 g) self-rising flour

1 teaspoon baking soda
(bicarbonate of soda)

¼ teaspoon salt

1 cup (5 oz/155 g) whole
raw almonds

FRONT: almond biscotti;
REAR: chocolate hazelnut biscotti
(page 236)

❖ Preheat an oven to 325°F (160°C/Gas Mark 3). Line a baking sheet with parchment (baking) paper.

❖ Use an electric mixer to beat the sugar, eggs, lemon zest, and almond extract until pale and frothy, about 2 minutes.

❖ Combine the all-purpose flour, self-rising flour, baking soda, and salt. Sift over the egg mixture, then use a large metal spoon to fold the ingredients together. Fold in the almonds. Mix to a soft dough. Do not overmix.

❖ Turn the dough onto a lightly floured surface and knead briefly until smooth. Divide the dough in half. Form each portion into a log, 8 inches (20 cm) long and 1½ inches (4 cm) thick. Place the logs on the prepared baking sheet, spacing them 4 inches (10 cm) apart.

❖ Bake for 45 minutes. Remove from the oven and allow to cool for 5 minutes. Use a serrated knife to cut each log into ½-inch (12-mm) thick slices, slightly on the diagonal.

❖ Return the slices to the baking sheet and bake for a further 15 minutes, turning after about 7 minutes, until crisp and lightly golden. Repeat with the remaining slices.

❖ Transfer to a wire rack to cool completely.

sesame fork
cookies

makes about 60 cookies

¾ cup (6 oz/185 g) butter or margarine, softened

1 cup (7 oz/220 g) packed brown sugar

1½ teaspoons baking powder

¼ teaspoon ground nutmeg

1 egg

3 tablespoons tahini (sesame paste) or peanut butter

1 teaspoon vanilla extract (essence)

1 cup (4 oz/125 g) whole-grain (whole-meal) flour

1⅔ cups (7 oz/220 g) all-purpose (plain) flour

⅓ cup (1 oz/30 g) sesame seeds

❖ Preheat an oven to 375°F (190°C/Gas Mark 4).

❖ In a large mixing bowl beat the butter or margarine with an electric mixer on medium to high speed for 30 seconds. Beat in the brown sugar, baking powder, and nutmeg. Beat in the egg, tahini or peanut butter, and vanilla. Beat in as much of the combined sifted flours as you can with the mixer. Stir in any remaining flour and the sesame seeds with a wooden spoon.

❖ Use lightly floured hands to shape the dough into 1-inch (2.5-cm) balls. Place the balls on ungreased baking sheets, spacing them 2 inches (5 cm) apart. Flatten each ball by pressing it with the floured tines of a fork in a crisscross pattern.

❖ Bake for 7–9 minutes, or until the cookies are lightly browned. Transfer to wire racks to cool.

date and walnut cookies

makes about 50

Dates give these cookies a
wonderful sweet touch.
Dried dates are sweeter,
richer, and more readily
available than fresh dates,
and will keep in an airtight
container for up to 6 months
in a cool, dry place.

1 cup (8 oz/250 g) butter or margarine, softened

1 cup (8 oz/250 g) raw sugar

1 egg

¾ cup (4½ oz/140 g) pitted dried dates, chopped

¾ cup (3 oz/90 g) chopped walnuts

grated zest (rind) of ½ orange

2 cups (8 oz/250 g) whole-grain (whole-meal) flour

2 teaspoons ground cinnamon

pinch of ground nutmeg

½ teaspoon baking soda (bicarbonate of soda),
dissolved in 1 teaspoon water

❖ Preheat an oven to 300°F (150°C/Gas Mark 2). Lightly butter baking sheets or line them with parchment (baking) paper.

❖ Use electric beaters to cream the butter or margarine and sugar until light and fluffy. Stir in the egg, dates, walnuts, and orange zest.

❖ Sift together the flour, cinnamon, and nutmeg. Add to the butter mixture along with the baking soda solution and mix well.

❖ Drop heaping teaspoons of the mixture onto the prepared baking sheets. Bake for 20 minutes or until lightly browned. Transfer to wire racks to cool.

recipe hint

An easy and effective way to butter baking sheets is to melt the butter first and then brush it on the baking sheets using a pastry brush.

crunchy
peanut cookies

makes about 24

If you love peanut butter cookies, try this delicious version which contains a combination of peanut butter and roasted peanuts.

¾ cup (6 oz/185 g) packed brown sugar

¾ cup (6 oz/185 g) butter, softened

⅔ cup (5 oz/155 g) peanut butter

1 teaspoon vanilla extract (essence)

1 cup (4 oz/125 g) self-rising flour

1 cup (4 oz/125 g) all-purpose (plain) flour

1¼ cups (6 oz/185 g) unsalted roasted peanuts, skinned and roughly chopped

❖ Preheat an oven to 375°F (190°C/Gas Mark 4). Lightly butter baking sheets or line them with parchment (baking) paper.

❖ In a bowl, beat the sugar, butter, peanut butter, and vanilla with an electric mixer on medium to high speed until light and creamy. Sift together the flours and add to the butter mixture, beating in as much flour as you can with the electric mixer. Beat in any remaining flour with a wooden spoon. Stir in the peanuts.

❖ Using lightly floured hands, roll heaping teaspoonfuls of the dough into balls about 1 inch (2.5 cm) in diameter, kneading each lightly to make the mixture come together. Place balls on prepared baking sheets, spacing them about 1 inch (2.5 cm) apart. Bake for 15–18 minutes or until golden brown.

❖ The cookies will still be quite soft; allow them to cool on the baking sheets for 5 minutes, then transfer to a wire rack to cool completely.

recipe variations

Try sprinkling the warm cookies with crushed nut brittle (recipes on page 212) or butter brittle for an extra crunchy twist.

walnut
anzacs

makes 24

Anzac biscuits, an Australian favorite, were so named during World War I. Eggs were rationed in Australia at the time, so these egg-less biscuits became a popular treat to send to men in the Australian and New Zealand Army Corps, who were known as ANZACS.

½ cup (4 oz/125 g) butter or margarine

2 tablespoons cornsyrup (golden syrup)

1 cup (4 oz/125 g) all-purpose (plain) flour, sifted

1 cup (7 oz/220 g) superfine (caster) sugar

¾ cup (2¼ oz/65 g) grated dried (desiccated) coconut

1 cup (4 oz/125 g) rolled oats

¼ cup (1 oz/30 g) chopped walnuts

1 teaspoon baking soda (bicarbonate of soda), dissolved in 2 tablespoons water

❖ Preheat an oven to 350°F (180°C/Gas Mark 4). Lightly butter baking sheets.

❖ In a small saucepan melt the butter or margarine and cornsyrup over low heat. Allow to cool.

❖ In a large bowl stir together the flour, sugar, coconut, oats, and walnuts. Add the baking soda solution to the butter mixture.

❖ Gradually add the butter mixture to the dry ingredients and stir until thoroughly combined.

❖ Roll the mixture into walnut-sized balls and place on the prepared baking sheets, spacing them well apart. Bake for 15 minutes for slightly chewy cookies, or 20 minutes for crisp cookies. Allow to cool on the baking sheets for 5 minutes, then transfer to a wire rack to cool completely.

recipe hint

Rolled oats are flat flakes that are made by steaming and rolling hulled oat grains. Rolled oats cook quicker than regular oats due to their flattened shape.

peanut butter
brittle
drops

makes about 60

If you love peanut butter cookies, try this delicious variation. The brittle pieces add a terrific crunchy-chewy texture to an old favorite.

1 cup (8 oz/250 g) butter or margarine, softened

1 cup (7 oz/220 g) packed brown sugar

1/2 cup (4 oz/125 g) granulated (white) sugar

1/2 teaspoon baking soda (bicarbonate of soda)

1 egg

1 cup (8 oz/250 g) crunchy peanut butter

1 teaspoon vanilla extract (essence)

2 1/2 cups (10 oz/315 g) all-purpose (plain) flour

1 1/3 cups (8 oz/250 g) butter brittle pieces (toffee bits)

✥ Preheat an oven to 375°F (190°C/Gas Mark 4). In a large mixing bowl beat the butter or margarine with an electric mixer on medium to high speed for 30 seconds. Add the brown sugar, granulated sugar, and baking soda; beat until combined. Beat in the egg, peanut butter, and vanilla. Beat in as much of the flour as you can with the mixer. Stir in any remaining flour with a wooden spoon. Stir in the butter brittle pieces.

✥ Drop rounded teaspoons of the dough onto ungreased baking sheets, spacing them 2 inches (5 cm) apart. Bake for 8–10 minutes, or until golden brown. Transfer to wire racks to cool.

recipe variations

For an extra nutty twist, try making these delectable cookies using the nut brittle recipes on pages 212–213 instead of butter brittle.

coffee walnut cookies

makes about 40

⅓ cup (3 oz/90 g) butter or margarine, softened

⅔ cup (5 oz/155 g) packed brown sugar

1 egg

2 teaspoons instant coffee granules, dissolved in 1 tablespoon boiling water

3 oz (90 g) finely chopped walnuts

1½ cups (6 oz/185 g) self-rising flour, sifted

❖ Preheat an oven to 375°F (190°C/Gas Mark 4). Lightly butter baking sheets or line them with parchment (baking) paper.

❖ Use an electric mixer to cream the butter and sugar until pale and creamy. Add the egg and coffee mixture and beat well. Stir in the walnuts and flour and beat lightly until well combined.

❖ Divide the mixture into 2 portions. Shape each into a log about 1½ inches (4 cm) in diameter, wrap in plastic wrap and chill for 30 minutes. (Place in tall glasses, then lay the glasses flat to help the logs keep their shape.)

❖ Cut the chilled logs into rounds ¼-inch (6-mm) thick and place on the prepared baking sheets, spacing them well apart. Bake for 10–12 minutes or until lightly browned. Transfer to wire racks to cool.

nut and raisin
squares

makes 24

½ cup (4 oz/125 g) butter, softened

1 cup (8 oz/250 g) sugar

2 eggs, lightly beaten

½ cup (2 oz/60 g) self-rising flour

½ cup (2 oz/60 g) all-purpose (plain) flour

½ teaspoon salt

3 tablespoons unsweetened cocoa powder

⅔ cup (4 oz/125 g) raisins

½ cup (2–3 oz/60–90 g) chopped nuts of your choice

1 teaspoon vanilla extract (essence)

❖ Preheat an oven to 350°F (180°C/Gas Mark 4). Lightly butter an 11 x 7-inch (28 x 18-cm) cake pan and line with parchment (baking) paper.

❖ Use an electric mixer to cream the butter and sugar together until pale and creamy. Add the eggs and beat thoroughly.

❖ Sift together the flours, salt, and cocoa and add to the butter mixture. Add the raisins, nuts, and vanilla and mix thoroughly. Spread into the prepared pan and bake for 45–50 minutes. Allow to cool in the pan, then cut into 24 squares.

crackers
and
savory
cookies

pretzel crackers

makes 48

2 cups (8 oz/250 g) all-purpose (plain) flour

1/4 teaspoon salt

ground black pepper

1/4 cup (1 oz/30 g) grated Parmesan cheese

3 tablespoons chilled butter, chopped

1 tablespoon sugar

1/2 cup (4 fl oz/125 ml) milk

1/4 cup (2 oz/60 g) coarse (kosher) salt

1/4 cup (2 oz/60 g) poppy seeds

❖ Preheat an oven to 400°F (200°C/Gas Mark 5). Line baking sheets with parchment (baking) paper.

❖ Place the flour, salt, pepper, and Parmesan in a food processor and process for 15 seconds. Add the butter and sugar and process until the mixture resembles bread crumbs. Transfer to a large bowl and add the milk. Use a wooden spoon to mix to a firm dough. Turn the dough onto a work surface and shape into a ball. Wrap in plastic wrap and refrigerate for 1 hour.

❖ Roll the dough between 2 sheets of parchment (baking) paper until 1/8-inch (3-mm) thick. Use a 2-inch (5-cm) cutter or a sharp knife to cut into shapes. Press coarse salt or poppy seeds on top of each cookie. Place on prepared baking sheets and bake for 10–15 minutes. Keep in an airtight container for up to 4 days.

mexican cheese savories

makes about 40

In Mexico, these cookies are commonly called *bocado* (bite) or *quesadillas* (because they are made of cheese). Dutch cheese, such as the Edam used in this recipe, became very popular in the port cities along the Gulf of Mexico when it arrived on European ships.

3½ oz (105 g) chilled butter, chopped

2 cups (8 oz/250 g) all-purpose (plain) flour

4 egg yolks

2 oz (60 g) lard, chopped

3½ oz (105 g) Edam cheese, grated

1 teaspoon salt, or to taste

¼ cup (2 oz/60 g) sugar (optional)

ground cinnamon, to taste (optional)

◈ Preheat an oven to 350°F (180°C/Gas Mark 4).

◈ On a work surface or in a large bowl, rub the butter into the flour with your fingers until the mixture resembles grains of rice. Make a well in the center and add the egg yolks, lard, cheese, and salt. Without kneading, combine all the ingredients into a dough.

◈ Divide the dough in half and flatten each portion using the palm of your hand or a rolling pin until it is ½ inch (12 mm) thick. Use a 1¼-inch (3-cm) round cookie cutter to cut out shapes. Gather together any scraps, flatten, and cut more rounds of dough. Repeat until all the dough is used.

◈ Place the rounds on ungreased baking sheets and bake for 30 minutes, but do not let them brown. (The surface of the cookies will bubble slightly while cooking.) Using a spatula, transfer to a plate. Sprinkle with the combined sugar and cinnamon, if desired. Serve warm or at room temperature.

food fact

Edam cheese is a semi-firm, uncooked, pressed cow's milk cheese that has a smooth yellow interior and bright red, waxy coating over a thin rind.

whole-grain grissini

makes about 50

*1 tablespoon (⅓ oz/10 g)
fresh yeast*

*⅔ cup (5 fl oz/160 ml)
lukewarm water*

*1 cup (4 oz/125 g) unbleached
all-purpose (plain) flour*

*1½ cups (6 oz/180 g)
whole-grain (whole-meal) flour*

1 cup (4 oz/125 g) semolina

1 teaspoon salt

*2 tablespoons extra virgin
olive oil*

❖ Preheat an oven to 400°F (200°C/Gas Mark 5).
Lightly butter baking sheets.

❖ In a small bowl dissolve the yeast in the water.

❖ In a large bowl combine the flours, ¾ cup (3 oz/
90 g) of the semolina, the salt, olive oil, and yeast
mixture. Knead for 10 minutes, until the dough is
smooth. Place in a floured bowl and set aside in a
warm place until the dough has doubled in volume.

❖ Punch down the dough and shape into long sticks
like thick pencils, each about 9 inches (23 cm) long and
½ inch (12 mm) thick. Roll each stick in the remaining
semolina. Place on the prepared baking sheets and
bake for 15 minutes, or until slightly golden. Transfer to
wire racks to cool. Serve warm or at room temperature.
The grissini are best eaten on the day they are made.

pita chips

makes about 40

4 pita pockets (Lebanese bread)

olive oil

paprika

❖ Preheat an oven to 375°F (190°C/Gas Mark 4).

❖ Cut each pita pocket into bite-sized triangles. Brush both sides of the bread with a little olive oil and sprinkle with paprika. Place in a single layer on a baking sheet and bake for 10–15 minutes, or until golden brown.

❖ Serve hot or at room temperature with drinks, dips, cheese, or as a snack. Store in an airtight container for up to 2 days. Recrisp in an oven preheated to 325°F (160°C/Gas Mark 3) for 5 minutes, if desired.

recipe variations

Brush the pita bread with a herbed oil of your choice (purchased, or choose a recipe on page 270) and then add a sprinkling of your favorite topping. Some good combinations include:

- Chile oil and finely chopped garlic
- Pesto and chopped pine nuts
- Olive or basil oil (page 270), chopped fried bacon, and finely grated cheese
- Chinese Stir-Fry Oil (page 271) and sesame seeds
- Chinese Stir-Fry Oil (page 271) and finely chopped green (spring) onion tops

ways with herbs

herb salt

Used instead of plain salt, herb salts can add interestingly different piquant flavors to a wide variety of savory cookies and crackers.

1 cup non-iodized sea salt or coarse (kosher) salt

1 cup (2 oz/60 g) packed fresh herbs, washed, thoroughly dried, and finely chopped; or 2 tablespoons dried herbs (basil, chives, dill, marjoram, oregano, rosemary, savory, thyme, and tarragon, alone or in combination, work especially well)

❖ Grind the salt and herbs together in a blender, or finely crumble the herbs by hand and mix them into the salt. Store in an airtight jar or place the mixture in a shaker.

herb butters

For tempting variations, replace ordinary butter in your savory cookies with herb butter. Create your own herb butter or follow the recipes below.

basic method

Most herb butter recipes call for sweet (unsalted) butter. (For less cholesterol, substitute margarine.) Soften at room temperature, then beat in the herbs and other seasonings by hand or with an electric mixer. For the best flavor, chill for at least 3 hours before serving.

Remember to wash herbs carefully before using them; soil and grit can hide in the small folds of leaves. Dry them thoroughly because even small amounts of water will affect the texture of the butter. For 1 tablespoon of fresh herbs, you may substitute 1½ teaspoons of dried herbs or, if you prefer, 1 teaspoon of seeds.

recipe variations

To make these herb butters, follow the basic method (left) and add the flavorings to 1 cup (8 oz/250 g) sweet (unsalted) butter or margarine, softened.

parsley butter
- ⅓ cup (½ oz/15 g) finely chopped fresh curly-leaf parsley
- 1 tablespoon fresh lemon juice
- 1 teaspoon Worcestershire sauce

garlic butter
- 4–6 cloves garlic, finely chopped

garlic and lemon butter
- 4 teaspoons finely chopped fresh garlic
- 2 teaspoons finely grated lemon zest (rind)
- 2 tablespoons fresh lemon juice

mixed herb butter
- ¼ cup (⅓ oz/10 g) each finely chopped fresh parsley and lovage
- 2 tablespoons finely chopped fresh thyme
- 1 tablespoon each finely chopped fresh sage, marjoram and garlic
- ½ teaspoon ground pepper

salt crackers

makes 60

This recipe is from the
Chianti region in Italy.
Serve these crackers
accompanied by olives
and some good wine
as an appetizer.

2 tablespoons (1/3 oz/10 g) fresh yeast

2/3 cup (5 fl oz/160 ml) lukewarm water

2 cups (8 oz/250 g) unbleached all-purpose (plain) flour

1 cup (4 oz/125 g) whole-grain (whole-meal) flour

1 tablespoon salt, plus extra for sprinkling

1/3 cup (2 1/2 fl oz/80 ml) extra virgin olive oil

❖ Preheat an oven to 400°F (200°C/Gas Mark 5). Lightly butter 2 large baking sheets.

❖ In a small bowl, dissolve the yeast in the water.

❖ In a large bowl, combine the flours, salt, 3 tablespoons of the olive oil, and the yeast mixture. Knead the dough for 5 minutes, until smooth and elastic. Shape the dough into a ball and place in a floured bowl. Set aside in a warm place until it has doubled in volume and the surface is slightly cracked.

❖ Divide the dough in half. Roll out 1 portion of dough on a floured surface to make a ¼-inch (5-mm) thick rectangle. Score it into 30 squares with a knife and prick each square with a fork. Brush with the remaining olive oil and sprinkle with a little extra salt. Carefully transfer to a prepared baking sheet. Repeat with the remaining portion of dough.

❖ Bake for 10 minutes. Remove from the oven and separate the squares, then bake for a further 5 minutes. Transfer to wire racks to cool completely.

storage hint

These crackers will keep in an airtight container for at least 2 weeks.

recipe variations

This recipe may be varied in many ways, for instance by adding very finely chopped fresh herbs (such as rosemary, sage, or thyme), or cumin or fennel seeds, to the dough. Or, you could use a herb salt (see recipes page 266) instead of the ordinary salt.

herbed oils

A light brushing of herbed oil can add a subtly delicious flavor to an otherwise plain savory cookie or cracker. The following oils are good on Pita Chips (page 267) or Salt Crackers (page 268). They are also great for basting broiled or grilled meats, in salad dressings, as a simple pasta sauce, for stir-frying vegetables, or added to soups.

basil oil

1 cup (1 oz/30 g) clean, fresh basil leaves

2 cups (16 fl oz/500 ml) good-quality olive oil

❖ Place the basil leaves in a sieve and plunge into boiling water for 1½ minutes. Remove immediately and place the leaves under cold running water. Turn the leaves onto a kitchen towel and pat until completely dry. Pack the blanched leaves into a sterilized jar and pour the oil over the top. Seal, label, and store in the refrigerator. Allow the flavor to infuse for at least 24 hours before using. This oil should be stored in the refrigerator. It will keep for up to 1 month.

❖ The leaves from this oil may also be used, a few at a time, especially when fresh basil is unavailable. They give a "fresher" taste than dried and can be used to replace fresh basil leaves in many recipes.

makes 2 cups (16 fl oz/500 ml)

chinese stir-fry oil

2 cups (16 fl oz/500 ml) groundnut
(peanut) oil

8 slices fresh ginger

5 cloves garlic

5–6 green (spring) onions, trimmed of roots
and 2 inches (5 cm) of green tops

❖ Heat the oil slowly in a heavy frying pan.
Crush the ginger and garlic with the wide
blade of a cleaver or knife and add to the
warm oil. Add the green onions. Heat
slowly for 8 minutes, or until the onions are
translucent. Allow the oil to cool and then
strain through coffee filter paper placed in a
funnel, into a sterilized storage bottle.

❖ Seal, label, and store in the refrigerator.
The oil should be refrigerated throughout
all stages of production, and will keep for
up to 1 month. The oil may become cloudy,
but will return to a clear state when warm.

makes 2 cups (16 fl oz/500 ml)

mediterranean herb oil

6 whole black peppercorns

6 sprigs fresh rosemary

3 bay leaves

2 sprigs fresh thyme

2 sprigs fresh oregano

1 qt (1 liter) extra virgin olive oil

❖ Place the peppercorns and herbs in a
sterilized 1-qt (1-liter) bottle. Add the olive
oil, ensuring that all the herbs are
completely covered. Seal, label, and store
in the refrigerator. Allow the flavors to
infuse for at least 10 days before using.
The oil should be refrigerated throughout
all stages of production, and will keep
for up to 1 month.

makes 1 qt (1 liter)

**Note: To sterilize jars, fill with boiling
water and set aside for 10 minutes. Pour
out the water and turn jars upside down
on clean kitchen towels to dry.**

cheese cookies

makes about 30

Deliciously cheesy, these cookies are perfect for a mid-afternoon snack or to serve as finger food when visitors drop in.

3/4 cup (3 oz/90 g) all-purpose (plain) flour, sifted

1 tablespoon dried bread crumbs

1/4 teaspoon cayenne pepper

1/4 teaspoon salt

1/4 cup (2 oz/60 g) chilled butter or margarine, chopped

1 cup (4 oz/125 g) grated cheese,
such as Parmesan, cheddar or jack cheese

1 egg

4–6 tablespoons (2–3 fl oz/60–90 ml) milk

❖ Preheat an oven to 350°F (180°C/Gas Mark 4). Lightly butter baking sheets or line them with parchment (baking) paper.

❖ In a bowl, combine the flour, bread crumbs, cayenne pepper, and salt. Use your fingers to rub in the butter or margarine until the mixture resembles bread crumbs. Add the cheese, egg, and enough of the milk to form a smooth dough.

❖ Roll out the dough on a lightly floured work surface or between 2 sheets of parchment (baking) paper until ¼ inch (6 mm) thick. Use a 2-inch (5-cm) cutter to cut the dough into desired shapes and place on the prepared baking sheets. Bake for 12–15 minutes or until golden brown.

recipe variation

For crisp biscuits, omit the bread crumbs and reduce the milk by 1–2 tablespoons.

water crackers

makes about 20

**Quick and easy to make,
these light, crisp water
crackers are the perfect
accompaniment to your
favorite dips or a
selection of cheeses.**

1 cup (4 oz/125 g) all-purpose (plain) flour

1/2 teaspoon baking powder

pinch of salt

1 oz (30 g) chilled butter, chopped

water, as needed

poppy seeds or sesame seeds (optional)

❖ Preheat an oven to 400°F (200°C/Gas Mark 5). Lightly butter baking sheets.

❖ Sift the flour, baking powder, and salt together into a bowl. Use your fingers to rub the butter into the flour mixture until evenly distributed. Stir in enough water to make a firm dough.

❖ Roll out the dough on a lightly floured work surface or between 2 sheets of parchment (baking) paper until ¼ inch (6 mm) thick. Use a 1-inch (2.5-cm) plain cookie cutter to cut the dough into rounds. Roll each round into a very thin circle or oval. Prick each cookie several times with a fork. Place on the prepared baking sheets, brush lightly with water and then sprinkle with the poppy seeds or sesame seeds, if desired. Bake until the cookies are puffed and golden, about 10 minutes. Transfer to wire racks to cool.

❖ Serve with savory toppings or cheese.

recipe variations

You can sprinkle the uncooked water crackers with a wlde variety of toppings. Try using sea salt, herb salt (recipe page 266), ground pepper, or dried herbs.

anchovy and olive cookies

makes about 35

With a combination of anchovies, olives, and cheese, these deliciously flavorsome cookies are always sure to impress.

1½ oz (45 g) can anchovy fillets, drained

milk, for soaking

3⅓ oz (100 g) all-purpose (plain) flour

3⅓ oz (100 g) chilled butter, cut into cubes

ground black pepper

1⅔ oz (50 g) Gruyère cheese, finely grated

1⅔ oz (50 g) grated Parmesan cheese

16 pitted black olives (preferably Kalamata), chopped

1 egg, beaten, for glazing

❖ Preheat an oven to 350°F (180°C/Gas Mark 4). Lightly grease 2 large baking sheets.

❖ Soak the anchovies in a little milk for 10 minutes to remove the excess salt. Drain and finely chop.

❖ Place the flour in the bowl of a food processor. Add the butter and pepper and process until combined and the mixture has a crumbly consistency.

❖ Use the pulse button to mix in the cheeses. Add the anchovies and olives and use the pulse button to mix to a rough dough. Take care not to overmix.

❖ Turn the dough onto a floured surface and knead briefly. Shape into a ball, wrap in plastic wrap and refrigerate for 20 minutes or until chilled.

❖ Roll the dough into a log, about 1½ inches (4 cm) thick. Cut into ½-inch (1-cm) rounds and place on the baking sheets, spacing them about ¾ inch (2 cm) apart. Brush with beaten egg and bake for 15 minutes or until firm and crisp. Transfer to a wire rack to cool.

food fact

Anchovies are tiny, silvery saltwater fish that are usually filleted and sold tinned in oil, or salt-cured. Their intense saltiness can be reduced by soaking them in milk for a few minutes, then draining and using as normal.

part
Two

techniques

making cookie dough ◈ measuring

mixing ◈ drop cookies ◈ bar cookies

cutout cookies ◈ sliced cookies

shaped and molded cookies

pressed cookies ◈ toppings

finishing touches ◈ storing

making cookie dough

No matter what kind of cookie you're baking, success depends upon three factors: using the best ingredients you can find; learning some basic skills (explained in this Part); and using the right equipment. For best results, use baking sheets that are made from shiny, heavyweight aluminum with low sides or with a lip on one edge. Baking pans with high, straight sides will block heat and cause the cookies to bake unevenly, while insulated sheets heat so slowly that cookies may require different baking times to those specified in these recipes. Also avoid dark sheets, as they absorb heat and may cause overbrowning. While the best procedure is to bake on the center rack of your oven, if you need to bake two sheets at once, place them on different levels and simply switch positions halfway through baking.

Before you begin baking, carefully read through the entire recipe and assemble all the ingredients and equipment that you will need. Always preheat your oven for at least 10 minutes before baking to ensure that it is at the correct temperature.

Make sure you keep all dry ingredients in airtight containers to protect them from moths and weevils, and to ensure they don't become rancid. Leavening agents, in particular, are best used before they reach their expiry date. Flour, nuts, and dried coconut can be kept in the refrigerator in hot or humid climates.

troubleshooting

cookies spread too much

• The baking sheet may have been warm when the cookie dough was placed on it.
• The baking sheet may have been too generously buttered.
• The oven wasn't preheated to the correct temperature.
• Diet margarine or vegetable oil spread may have been used instead of butter or regular margarine.

cookies didn't spread enough

• The cookie dough could have been overmixed.
• The oven wasn't preheated to the correct temperature.

cookies stuck to the baking sheet

• The cookies may be undercooked.
• The baking sheet may not have been greased sufficiently or it may have been warm when the dough was placed on it.
• The baked cookies may have been left on the baking sheet for too long.

basic equipment

Having the right tools for the job will make baking easier and more streamlined. You will need:

• an electric mixer
• a food processor
• large and small bowls
• measuring cups and jugs
• measuring spoons
• measuring scales
• wooden spoons
• metal spoons
• metal and rubber spatulas
• knives
• cutting board
• baking sheets
• wire racks
• parchment (baking) paper or waxed (greaseproof) paper
• oven mitt
• clean kitchen towels

measuring ingredients

When measuring small amounts of liquid or dry ingredients, use measuring spoons that are sold in standard sets, not just any spoons that you use to eat or serve food with. Measure liquids by pouring them into the spoon until the spoon is full. Measure dry ingredients by pouring or scooping them into the spoon until the spoon is full, then level them with a small metal spatula or knife.

When measuring larger amounts of dry ingredients, use measuring cups that are sold in standard sets, not regular cups or glasses. When measuring larger amounts of liquids, use glass or transparent plastic measuring cups or jugs that have a spout.

flour

Before spooning the flour into the measuring cup, stir it lightly with a fork in the canister to lighten it. Then, fill the cup with flour, but don't pack it down— just tap the cup lightly. Level the flour by sweeping across the top with a small metal spatula or a knife. Unless the recipe calls for it, there is no need to sift all-purpose flour. If, however, you do need to sift flour, always do this after you have measured it.

sugar

When measuring granulated (white) sugar or superfine (caster) sugar, spoon it into a dry measuring cup, then level it off using a small metal spatula or a knife.

When measuring brown sugar, spoon it into a dry measuring cup so it rises in a mound slightly above the rim. Press the brown sugar firmly into the cup with your hand. (This is what is meant by "packed" brown sugar.) To unmold, turn upside down; the sugar will still hold the shape of the cup.

vegetable shortening

Rinsing the measuring cup with boiling water before adding shortening will make it easier to remove later. Fill the measuring cup with vegetable shortening. Press the shortening firmly into the cup with a rubber spatula. Level it off by sweeping across the rim with the spatula or a knife.

butter or margarine

Don't have the butter or margarine too soft or it won't cut cleanly and accurately. With a sharp knife, cut through the butter or margarine following the measurement guidelines printed on the wrapping paper. Allow it to soften fully (but not to melt) before making the cookie dough. Don't use margarine when a recipe, such as shortbread, calls specifically for butter. It is necessary to use chilled butter for rubbing into flour and when mixing with dry ingredients in a food processor.

liquids

Place a glass or transparent plastic liquid measuring cup or jug on a counter or tabletop. Add the liquid. For the greatest accuracy, it is best to check the measurement at eye level rather than from above.

Sticky liquids, such as honey or molasses, will pour out smoothly if the measuring cup is first brushed lightly with oil, or dipped in hot water for a few seconds and then wiped dry.

mixing cookie dough

The ingredients you use, and their quantities, are very important when making cookie dough. The key ingredients in cookies are flour, fat, baking powder or baking soda (bicarbonate of soda), sugar, eggs, and other liquids. All these ingredients have a special role to play, and doing something as small as using baking powder instead of baking soda (bicarbonate of soda) or all-purpose (plain) flour instead of self-rising flour can make a big difference to the finished result. Making sure that you measure your ingredients carefully will also help ensure your cookies turn out perfectly. Too much or too little of an ingredient can upset the overall balance of the recipe.

Although cookies may not be as delicate as cakes, mixing still plays an important part in their overall success. Many cookies are made by first creaming butter and sugar, then adding the other ingredients bit by bit until they are all combined. Creaming helps to incorporate air into the batter, making it light and fluffy. Overmixing dough can make the resulting cookies tough, so it is best to mix just until the liquid and dry ingredients are combined and no longer.

The fats most often used when baking cookies are butter, margarine, shortening, and oil. Be careful when substituting one for another in a recipe as it may affect the finished result, causing the cookies to spread too much or too little, or not have the desired texture. Flavorings may be substituted, such as nuts or dried fruit, but key ingredients are best left as they are.

steps for success

mixing in ingredients

Using an electric mixer, prepare the dough according to the recipe directions up to the point of adding the flour. The dough will still stir easily at this stage and won't strain the motor of the mixer. Scrape down the sides of the bowl once or twice with a rubber spatula, then continue mixing.

adding the flour

Add the flour gradually, beating in as much as you can using the electric mixer (the dough will become stiff). Some portable mixers do not have motors that are powerful enough to incorporate all of the flour; if your mixer begins to strain or cut out, stir in any remaining flour by hand with a wooden or metal spoon. Mix only until the dough is a homogeneous mixture with no streaks of flour showing.

cookie dough tip

The temperature of a cookie dough can also play a role in determining its success. Some recipes call for doughs to be chilled, so they can be sliced or cut into shapes. However, if you are cooking on a warm day or you are doing a lot of baking and your kitchen is hot, it is a good idea to chill any cookie dough before using. This will prevent the cookies spreading too much during baking.

making drop cookies

Making drop cookies is a very simple craft. No artistry is required, only a gentle push to transfer the dough from the spoon to the baking sheet. As they bake, the soft, chunky mounds spread and settle into irregular rounds with homely appeal that are perfect with a good cup of coffee or a frosty glass of chilled milk.

Not only are drop cookies easy to prepare, but they are wonderfully versatile. By varying a few ingredients or adjusting the proportions, you can change this kind of cookie dramatically. Their texture can be chewy, or soft and tender. Drop cookies are not always made from a traditional dough: Amaretti (page 238), for example, are Italian chewy meringues that are made from a frothy mixture of egg whites, sugar, and ground almonds.

steps for success

stirring in ingredients

After mixing the basic dough (see page 284), beat in as much of the flour as you can with the mixer. Then, mix in remaining flour and other ingredients with a wooden or metal spoon.

dropping dough

Scoop up the dough with a small metal spoon. With the back of another spoon or a rubber spatula, push the dough onto the prepared baking sheet.

testing for doneness

When they are done, the cookies will be lightly browned underneath. Check by lifting one cookie with a spatula to see the color of its underside. The dough should also feel set.

cooling on a rack

When the cookies have finished baking, remove them from the oven and set them aside on the baking sheet for a few minutes to cool and firm a little. Then, use a metal spatula that is big enough to support a whole cookie to transfer them to a wire rack to cool completely.

basic equipment

Use a large bowl and wooden or metal spoon for drop-cookie dough, plus smaller bowls for additions such as nuts or dried fruit. Two tablespoons or teaspoons are all you need to transfer the dough to the baking sheet. Transfer cookies to a wire rack using a wide metal spatula.

making bar cookies

Mix, bake, serve. Bar cookies are as basic as that. But here, basic means easy, not bland or boring. Brownies, (like the delectable Choc-Coconut Brownies on page 198) fall into this category, and it's hard to imagine a more delicious dessert or a more popular one. Unlike drop cookies, which are made from a soft dough, bar cookies are made from a fluid batter that needs a baking pan with sides for support.

For best results, spread the batter evenly in the pan, so that the finished bar isn't thin and dried out in one corner, and thick and undercooked in another. Let the bar cool in the pan, then run a sharp, thin-bladed knife between the bar and the inside edge of the pan. Turn the bar out onto a wire rack and ice, then cut into uniform portions, such as squares, rectangles, triangles, or diamonds. Alternatively, you can cut the bar into pieces first, run the knife between the bar and the inside edge of the pan, and then use a spatula that is large enough to support each piece to transfer the pieces to a wire rack.

steps for success

preparing the pan

If the baking pan must be greased, do it as the first step in the recipe. Coat a piece of paper towel or waxed (greaseproof) paper with butter or shortening, then apply in a thin, even layer on base and sides of pan.

If you prefer, you can use parchment (baking) paper. This has a nonstick coating and doesn't need to be greased. Use a large piece that will cover the base of the pan and extend over the two long sides. To remove the cooled bar, run a knife between the short sides of the pan and the bar cookie, then use the overhanging parchment paper to lift the bar from the pan.

combining ingredients

If the batter calls for a melted ingredient, allow it to cool slightly before beating in the eggs. Then, gently stir in the remaining ingredients, such as flour and baking powder, with a wooden or metal spoon.

spreading batter in pan

Spread the batter in a smooth, even layer across the base of the pan with a rubber spatula or the back of a wooden spoon. If the pan has sharp corners, make sure the batter fills each one completely.

testing for doneness

Toward the end of baking time, begin to check for doneness. Depending on the recipe, look for the batter to be set, the edges to be browned, or the mixture to pull away slightly from the sides of the pan.

bar cookie hints

Some bar cookie recipes are so simple and quick that the batter is mixed in a saucepan and then spooned straight into a baking pan.

See page 291 for the equipment that you will need to make bar cookies, and also for instructions on how to cut bar cookies.

bar cookies with a crust

Multilayered bar cookies have great visual appeal. Although they look complex, they are simple to assemble, which means maximum results from minimum effort. Most bar cookie crusts are quickly tossed together with a pastry blender or a spoon and are formed into a layer in the pan with your fingers.

If the filling for a multilayered bar cookie is very liquid, the crust must be prebaked so that it won't become soggy. When cutting bar cookies and bar cookies with a crust, you will get the neatest results if you mark off your lines with a simple grid. For either squares or diamonds, use toothpicks as guides for your cutting lines. A perfect square cut in half will make a perfect triangle. For a more generous triangle, cut rectangles in half.

steps for success

cutting in butter or margarine
Use a fork to stir together flour, sugar, and salt until thoroughly blended. Cut chilled butter or margarine into pieces and cut into the flour mixture with a pastry blender, using an up-and-down motion, until the mixture is crumbly.

pressing into pan
Transfer the crust mixture to a baking pan (if the dough is rich, there is no need to grease the pan first). Push the dough around with your hands until it covers the base of the pan in an even layer. Be sure to fill the corners.

spreading filling evenly
While the crust is briefly baking, prepare the filling. Remove the crust from the oven,

place it on a wire rack, and pour over the filling. Spread it out evenly using a rubber spatula so that every part of the hot crust is covered.

cutting bar cookies in pan

Let the bar cookie cool completely in the pan before cutting it. Then, mark cutting lines with toothpicks inserted around the inside edge of the pan. Cut into pieces with a small, sharp knife, using the toothpicks as guides.

cutting triangles

To create triangles, first cut the bar cookie into squares and then cut each square in half diagonally, working from one side of the pan to the other.

cutting diamonds

As instructed above, place toothpicks around the rim of the pan to mark where you will cut. Divide the cookie lengthwise into long strips, then cut the strips into diamonds by making diagonal cuts from one side of the pan to the other.

basic equipment

You will need a mixing bowl and electric mixer for regular bar cookies, or a mixing bowl and pastry blender for multilayered bar cookies. You will aslo need a rubber spatula to transfer the batter to a baking pan and to spread fillings, and a sharp knife and toothpicks to cut the bar cookie into even pieces.

making cutout cookies

A buttery cookie shaped like a little boy, or a cookie kitten with its tail tucked under, is more than just a confection. It is an edible example of cookie artistry. Some cookie shapes are formed with a cutter, others are created with a ruler and knife. All are made from a rich, pliable dough that must be chilled for easier handling, an advantage because it can be made several days ahead. When ready, place dough on a lightly floured work surface or between two sheets of parchment (baking) paper to prevent it sticking. Roll the dough out into a thin, even sheet.

Now the fun begins. There are countless cookie cutter shapes for every occasion. Be sure to select cutters that have sharp edges and patterns that are free of tiny details, such as little ears or skinny tails that might break off as the dough drops from the cutter.

To make the most out of a piece of dough, view it like an uncut puzzle and space the shapes as close together as you can. Knead the scraps and then reroll to use up any remaining dough. After baking, let the cookies cool briefly on the baking sheet, then transfer to a wire rack with a large spatula that can fully support each cookie. Let the hot baking sheets cool before using them again, or the dough will spread out of shape.

steps for success

chilling dough

Prepare the dough and then divide it into two equal portions; flatten each slightly. Tear off two large squares of plastic wrap. Tightly wrap each piece of dough in plastic wrap and refrigerate until the dough is easy to handle, about 1–3 hours, depending on the recipe.

Chilled dough is easier to roll and won't stick to the rolling pin. The dough can be kept in the fridge for up to 1 week.

measuring thickness

On a lightly floured surface, roll out a portion of dough until it reaches the thickness instructed in the recipe (keep the remaining half chilled until needed). Measure the dough with a ruler to check that it is of uniform thickness.

cutting out cookies

Dip the cutting edge of the cookie cutter in flour. Set the cutter on the dough and press straight down with equal pressure all the way around so the entire pattern is cut out.

moving cookie to sheet

Slide a large, wide spatula under the cookie and transfer it to a baking sheet. Leave some room between the cookies because they will expand as they bake.

rerolling scraps

When as many cookies as possible have been cut out of the dough, gather the scraps with lightly floured hands and then gently knead. Reroll the dough until 1 inch (2.5 cm) thick and cut out more cookies.

basic equipment

You will need a baking sheet, wire rack, mixing bowl, wide metal spatula, plastic wrap, ruler, rubber spatula, rolling pin, and assorted cookie cutters.

making sliced cookies

S liced cookies, also called refrigerator cookies and icebox cookies, are the ultimate in convenience. You make the dough when you have the time, roll it into a log, wrap in plastic and store in the refrigerator for up to 1 week, or the freezer for up to 1 month. When you want cookies in a hurry, all you have to do is slice them and bake them. You don't even have to use the whole log at once. Just cut off what you need and return the rest to the refrigerator or freezer. Very cold dough cuts into thin slices more easily, so you get the added advantage of being able to make wafer-thin cookies in no time at all.

When unexpected guests arrive, when your child brings home a friend from school, or when you've run out of ideas for dessert, you can remove your ready-made log of cookie dough from the fridge or freezer and slice your way out of trouble.

Sliced-cookie dough is too soft to cut initially, much like the mixture used for cutout cookies. The two doughs are similar in their early stages. Both have similar consistencies and are refrigerated, but they differ in the way they are shaped. While cutouts are punched out of a rolled sheet of dough, sliced cookies are cut from a solid log of dough.

To add texture and flavor, the log of dough can be rolled in chopped nuts before it is baked, if desired. A nicely rounded shape is also an important part of the visual appeal of sliced cookies. If the dough flattens as you slice it, roll it back into a log and chill it again for 5–10 minutes.

steps for success

shaping dough

Divide the dough in half. Place each half on a sheet of plastic wrap large enough to fully enclose it. Roll the dough into a log inside the wrap. Seal the ends airtight.

storing log of dough

To keep the log nicely rounded, chill it inside a tall, narrow glass. If the log is longer than your glass, cut it into several portions and store it in several glasses.

slicing cookies

Unwrap the chilled log of dough. Cut it into ¼-inch (6-mm) thick slices with a sharp knife. Always use a knife with a thin, sharp blade and slice with a back-and-forth sawing motion, not a downward swipe.

testing for doneness

Bake in an oven preheated to 375°F (190°C/Gas Mark 4) until the edges are firm and the cookies are lightly browned underneath, about 8–10 minutes, or as the recipe instructs. Transfer the cookies to a wire rack to cool completely.

basic equipment

You will need a baking sheet, wire rack, cutting board, plastic wrap, tall glass/es, rubber or metal spatula, and sharp knife.

making shaped and molded cookies

Cookie dough for shaping and molding is buttery and pliable, yet more tolerant of handling than most other cookie doughs. It can be rolled, twisted, and formed into shapes, such as twisted pretzels or fluted cups, that cannot be created with a cutter. This kind of dough also holds an impression. You can imprint it with simple linear patterns such as the familiar crisscross used on Sesame Fork Cookies (page 248), or mold it to make a cookie with a handsome rope edge and center medallion, such as Shortbread (page 108).

Shaped and molded cookies look best when all the cookies in a batch are similar in size and shape. They will also bake more evenly if all are the same size.

Take a little time to become familiar with this type of dough so you can develop just the right touch for each recipe, whether it's a delicate chocolate-dipped pirouette (page 218) or a spicy, coiled Cinnamon Snail (page 104). The skills needed to make balls and ropes from cookie dough are explained in this section and are important basics that you will use often.

steps for success

shaping balls

Divide the dough into equal portions of about 1 tablespoon each. Roll each portion between the palms of your hands until it is nicely rounded and smooth all over. Place the balls on lightly greased cookie sheets.

pressing with a fork

Leave a fair amount of space between balls of dough. Flatten cookies with the tines of a fork, then press again perpendicular to the first marks to create crisscross lines.

making ropes

Divide the log of dough into 2-inch (5-cm) pieces. Roll each piece into a thin, 8-inch (20-cm) long rope by working it back and forth with your fingers on a lightly floured surface. As you roll the dough, work from the center out to lengthen it.

shaping true pretzels

To make a true pretzel, form a circle with a rope of dough, crossing one end over the other about 1 inch (2.5 cm) from each end. Twist once where the rope overlaps (the dough will spiral around, and the rope's ends will extend slightly beyond the twist).

After the overlapped ends have been twisted once, lift them and place on the opposite edge of the circle. Press the ends with your fingers to attach to the dough.

shaping simple pretzels

This shape is similar to a true pretzel and is easier to accomplish. Lay a rope of dough on a baking sheet. Form a circle by crossing one end over the other, overlapping about 1 inch (2.5 cm) from ends. Bring ends down to opposite edge of circle. Press to seal.

basic equipment

Because your hands do much of the shaping, you only need a baking sheet, mixing bowl, measuring spoon, cutting board, fork, and knife.

making
pressed
cookies

Pressed, or "spritz", cookies are an old Scandinavian speciality, but they have become a favorite in many other countries, too. Most cookie presses are simple devices that operate with either a lever-and-ratchet system or a rotating screw-top (an electric press is also available, but is a little more difficult to find). A removable coupler at the bottom of the container holds your choice of interchangeable design plates and, in some cases, plain- or star-shaped nozzles.

To use, secure the plate or nozzle, pack the dough into the container, and force it through the press onto a baking sheet. Out come little wreaths, miniature trees, dainty butterflies, delicate flowers, ridged ribbons, or any of the dozens of patterns created by the manufacturer. The press does all the work and does it perfectly. All you need to do is make the dough, choose the design, and bake the result. What could be simpler, and more effective?

As the shapes of the cookies themselves are so decorative, the only finishing touch you may like to consider could be a light sprinkling of glittering sugar crystals, a scattering of finely chopped nuts, colored sprinkles, nonpareils, or adding a delicious chocolate tint to the cookie dough. Always use room-temperature dough, as chilled dough is too stiff to push through the cookie press easily.

steps for success

putting plate in holder

Unscrew the holder from the bottom of the cookie press. Place a plate in the holder with the correct side facing up (as specified by the manufacturer's directions). Make sure the plate rests flat in the holder.

packing press with dough

Scoop up the cookie dough using a rubber spatula and then pack it into the container of the cookie press. Be careful not to leave any large air holes in the dough or the shapes will distort when they are pressed out. Screw on the holder and plate or tip.

forcing dough through press

For all shapes except ribbons (see directions top right), hold the cookie press straight down on an ungreased baking sheet. Force the dough through (it will stick to the cookie sheet) and then release the pressure just before you lift the press off the cookie.

making ribbons

Hold the cookie press at an angle. Draw the press along the ungreased baking sheet in a straight line as you force out the dough. Lift up the press when the ribbons are the desired length.

making diagonal ribbons

Press out long strips of dough onto the baking sheet. Use a sharp knife to cut the strips at an angle, being careful not to cut too deeply so you will not mark the baking sheet.

basic equipment

For pressed cookies, you need the standard equipment for making and baking dough, plus an easy-to-operate press that comes with an assortment of removable design plates.

toppings
and meringues

P lain cookies have their own special place in our hearts, but decorated cookies, whether simply iced or lavishly embellished, have a particular appeal. This section gives tips on handling and melting chocolate, making meringue toppings, and drizzling icings.

Chocolate, sugar, and eggs: these three ingredients turn up time and again in every type of cookie, whether dropped from a spoon, baked in a pan, piped from a pastry bag, or formed with a cutter. The steps on these pages explain how to use these popular ingredients to give your cookies that extra special touch. Not only will you come across these techniques in recipes throughout the book, you'll also find them used in almost all types of baking, so they are good tricks to know.

You will learn how to melt chocolate to flavor dough or to decorate it, to make that miraculous cloud-like product of egg white and sugar called meringue, how to apply icing in a network of fine lines (a technique known as drizzling), and how to pipe icing or melted chocolate from a heavy-duty plastic bag instead of using a piping bag with nozzle or a teaspoon.

Refer to the section on Finishing Touches (page 304) for more ideas on decorating and presenting cookies, whether for special occasions, gifts, or just for fun.

chocolate

melting chocolate

Great care should be taken when melting chocolate. It burns very easily and this makes the flavor bitter, and if overheated, it becomes hard and granular. Be careful not to let even the slightest amount of steam or water come into contact with the chocolate, or it will "seize" (stiffen and solidify). Nothing can be done once this has happened; you will have to throw the chocolate out and start again. This problem does not arise if a recipe calls for chocolate to be combined with water, butter, or shortening, and then melted.

There are several ways to melt chocolate:
1. To melt chocolate on the stovetop, use a double boiler or a heatproof bowl that fits snugly over a saucepan. Put a small amount of water in the bottom part of the boiler or in the saucepan; do not allow the water to touch the bottom of the bowl or top boiler.

Bring the water to the boil and then remove from the heat. Place the chocolate in the bowl or top boiler and return the saucepan to the heat, if necessary, stirring to melt the chocolate. Do not cover the bowl; this will cause steam to condense on the lid and fall into the chocolate, making it "seize."

2. Another method, particularly useful when melting only a small amount of chocolate, is to put the chocolate (and butter or shortening, if using) in a heatproof bowl over (but not touching) hot water. Let the chocolate stand, stirring it occasionally, until it has melted.

3. The dry heat of the microwave oven is ideal for melting chocolate. Place the chocolate pieces (and butter or shortening, if using) in a glass dish and microwave on high (100%) for 1–3 minutes, stirring 1–2 times during melting depending on the amount to be melted. The chocolate will retain its shape, so stir it to melt it fully.

toppings and meringues

4. This method uses a heavy-duty plastic bag. Place the chocolate (and butter or shortening, if using) in the bag and push the contents to one corner. Tie the bag just above the mixture, then set the bag in a bowl of warm water to melt. Rub the bag to blend the contents. This method is useful when decorating cookies, as you can just snip a tiny piece from the corner of the bag to create an icing bag with which you can drizzle the chocolate over the cookies.

drizzling chocolate or icing

Arrange cooled cookies on a wire rack over waxed (greaseproof) paper. Fill a small spoon with icing or melted chocolate. Move the spoon back and forth over each cookie to create fine lines. Let the icing or chocolate flow off the spoon in a ribbon.

You can also drizzle icing or chocolate with a fork or, for a more regular pattern, with a pastry bag and small round tip, or with a plastic bag (see method 4, above).

making meringue

using egg whites

Always bring the egg whites to room temperature before using them to make meringues. Cold egg whites incorporate less air than those at room temperature.

adding sugar

With an electric mixer on medium speed, beat the egg whites until they are white and foamy and the tips of the peaks bend over when the beaters are lifted out (soft peaks). Gradually add the sugar, 1 tablespoon at a time, until the mixture is smooth and glossy and the sugar has completely dissolved.

beating to stiff peaks

Continue beating the egg whites and sugar until the mixture begins to stiffen. The meringue is ready when it looks smooth and glossy, the sugar has completely dissolved, and the mixture forms peaks

that hold their shape when the beaters
are lifted (stiff peaks).

making icings

Icings are simple to make and can turn a
plain cookie into a special treat in no time.
The most simple icings are made using
confectioners' (icing) sugar, butter, and
milk or water. Flavorings can be added,
such as vanilla extract (essence), lemon
juice, orange juice or almond extract
(essence). Or, food coloring can be used
to color the icing.

basic equipment

To prepare toppings and meringue,
you will need:

- electric mixer
- large and small mixing bowls
- spoons for measuring and stirring
- wire rack
- double boiler or heatproof bowl
- small saucepan
- small spoons for drizzling
- heavy-duty small plastic bags
- piping bags and assorted nozzles
- waxed (greaseproof) paper

meringue hint

Moisture is a meringue's greatest enemy.
Try to avoid making meringues on humid
or rainy days, and avoid making them
when you are cooking other dishes as
moisture in the air will prevent them
from drying completely.

finishing touches

There are myriad ways you can give cookies a special finishing touch, whether you're serving them at a special occasion, giving them as a gift, or taking them to sell at a school fair.

Icing in different flavors, colors, and designs; a coating of melted chocolate, chopped nuts, or coconut; or even decorative packaging can all help to transform cookies into works of art. In this section, you'll find plenty of ideas to help you get started. Use them to guide you and to give you inspiration, and there will be no limits to your creativity.

Remember, iced cookies and those with toppings do not always store well, so try to decorate cookies as close as possible to serving. For information on storing cookies, see page 304.

using icings

Icing can be spread over cookies with a flat-bladed knife, painted on cookies using a pastry brush, drizzled over cookies, or you can simply dip the cookie in the icing. You can press small candies into the icing before it sets to make pretty patterns, or when the first coating has set, you can apply more icing to draw stripes, spirals, dots, or animal faces. For information on making icings, see page 303.

using chocolate

For information on melting chocolate, see pages 301–302. Cookies can be dipped in melted chocolate, or you can drizzle the chocolate over them. Just like icing, you can apply more chocolate once the first layer has set to make a variety of patterns. Using two different types of chocolate, such as semisweet (plain) and white chocolate gives a striking effect and tastes delicious. Try dipping one end of the cookie in semisweet chocolate and the other end in white chocolate, or dip the entire cookie in white chocolate and then drizzle it with semisweet chocolate. The options are endless, and all taste fabulous!

chopped nuts

Chopped nuts are a great way to spice up cookies. Cookies can be rolled in or sprinkled with finely chopped nuts before baking, or you can sprinkle the cookies with nuts straight after dipping them in melted chocolate, before the chocolate has set. For information on toasting, skinning, and peeling nuts, see page 211.

dusting cookies

Perhaps the simplest way to give cookies a quick make-over is to dust them. You can use confectioners' (icing) sugar or granulated sugar; a combination of

confectioners' sugar and unsweetened cocoa powder; or ground cinnamon and sugar. Use a fine-mesh sieve to ensure the cookies are covered lightly and evenly. Place paper shapes on the cookies before dusting them to create patterns, if you like. Or try dusting just half of each cookie.

party ideas

There are many ways you can decorate cookies for children's parties, using the techniques and ingredients mentioned above. Try using icing to write each child's name on a cookie and then place the cookies on the table to indicate who sits where. Or, use different colored icings to draw the children's faces on the cookies and let them work out which cookie belongs to which child.

Cutout cookies are always popular with children, and when decorated with melted chocolate or icing, make great prizes for games. Choose a packaging idea from page 306 to wrap a few cookies at a time.

finishing touches

packaging ideas

wrapping paper

This is the easiest (and often the cheapest) way to package cookies. Be sure to wrap the cookies in plastic wrap or place them in a small, clear, airtight plastic bag before wrapping to keep them fresh. Try to use a variety of colors and textures to keep the packaging interesting. Tissue paper, clear or colored cellophane, and glossy printed papers all look terrific. Even plain brown paper and newspaper can be dressed up to look exciting and unusual.

boxes and bags

You can buy pretty, colorful boxes and paper or cardboard bags from gift shops. For a cheaper option, you could simply paint old boxes you have at home, or wrap them in colorful paper. Tying a pretty wide ribbon around the side of the box will help give it an elegant touch.

ribbons

Ribbons come in such a wide range of beautiful colors and textures, and are an inexpensive way to dress up packaged cookies. Tie them around boxes, around the tops of bags, or use them to secure wrapping paper. You can tie them in big looping bows or just let them hang down with the ends cut on the diagonal.

baked cookie tip

As soon as possible after removing cookies from the oven, lift them onto a wire rack to cool. Some cookies need a minute or two to firm up, but if you leave them on the baking sheet for too long, they will continue to cook and sometimes they will stick. If this happens, return the baking sheet to the oven for a couple of minutes to soften the cookies again.

storing cookies

Although it is a rare batch that lasts more than a few days without being devoured down to the very last crumb, cookies can become stale quickly unless protected against air or excess moisture. Proper storage also prevents them from breakage or other damage.

Let the cookies cool completely, then arrange in single layers in an airtight container. (Select a storage container that allows easy access to the cookies inside.) If the cookies are soft, place a sheet of waxed (greaseproof) paper between each layer. Seal the airtight container. They will keep at room temperature for up to 3 days.

Store soft and crisp cookies separately, or the crisp ones will absorb moisture from the others and become soft themselves. On the other hand, you can revive soft cookies that have dried out and hardened by placing a wedge of apple or a slice of bread on a piece of waxed (greaseproof) paper and setting it on top of the cookies in the closed container. Remove after 1 day.

If you prefer, leave bar cookies in their baking pan, covered tightly with plastic wrap or aluminum foil.

For longer storage, freeze unfrosted cookies in airtight heavy-duty freezer bags or freezer containers. They will stay fresh for up to 6 months. When needed, thaw the cookies (if they need to be recrisped, follow the method below) and then decorate.

To recrisp cookies, place them in an oven preheated to 325°F (160°C/Gas Mark 3) for 5–7 minutes. Transfer the cookies to a wire rack to firm.

glossary

bananas

Tropical bananas are usually yellow-skinned, with creamy, sweet flesh, although some varieties have red skin and pink flesh. Use slightly overripe bananas for baking. Green or unripe bananas will ripen in a few days at room temperature.

butter brittle pieces

Brittle (or brickle) is a golden-brown, buttery, hard toffee. Add packaged brittle pieces to cookie doughs and batters as directed in the recipe. Available in the confectionery section of most supermarkets, these are sometimes called "toffee bits."

chocolate

Several chocolate types are commonly used in baking. *Sweet (milk) chocolate* contains at least 15 percent pure cocoa mass (the compound that gives chocolate its flavor), extra cocoa butter, and sugar. *Unsweetened (bitter) chocolate* is pure cocoa mass with no sugar or flavoring, while *unsweetened cocoa powder* is pure cocoa mass with very little cocoa butter. Because it lacks cocoa mass, *white chocolate* is not considered a true chocolate product, although it does contain cocoa butter. Chopped *semisweet (plain or dark) chocolate* is interchangeble with semisweet (plain or dark) chocolate chips. Store chocolate, well wrapped, in a cool, dry place for up to 4 months.

coconut

The dried flesh of the coconut is available in a number of forms, including grated (desiccated), shredded, and flaked, either sweetened or unsweetened. It will keep for months if stored airtight.

coffee

Instant coffee granules and instant espresso powder are preferred for baking because of their intense flavor and because they blend easily into batters, doughs, and liquid mixtures. They will keep indefinitely if stored in an airtight container.

cooking fats

Butter, margarine, and solid vegetable shortening make cookies tender. *Butter* and *margarine* are interchangeable in almost all recipes. However, margarine made from 100 percent vegetable oil will make a very soft cookie dough that may require a longer chilling time to prevent the dough from spreading too much during baking. Use only regular margarine, not diet, whipped, or liquid forms. *Shortening* is a vegetable-oil-based fat that is manufactured to stay solid at room temperature. Butter and margarine will keep for 1 month, well wrapped in the refrigerator, or up to 6 months in the freezer. Store shortening at room temperature for up to 1 year.

cream cheese

Cream cheese, a mixture of cow's cream and milk, has a smooth, spreadable consistency and mild, slightly tangy flavor. It is available in bricks and in bulk. Refrigerate and use within one week of purchase.

dried fruit

Drying intensifies the natural flavor of fruit, concentrates its sweetness, and preserves it. Dried fruits such as dates, apricots, raisins, sultanas (golden raisins) and figs are a favorite addition to cookies. Unopened packages of dried fruit will stay wholesome almost indefinitely. Once opened, transfer the contents to a plastic bag or glass jar and store in the refrigerator.

eggs

Cookies acquire flavor, tenderness, richness, and structure from eggs, although not every cookie recipe uses eggs. Shell color—brown or white—is purely superficial; there is no difference in quality. Refrigerate in the carton for up to 5 weeks.

flour

Wheat flour gives cookies their structure. *All-purpose flour* has a medium protein content that makes it suitable for most baking uses. *Wholemeal flour* is coarsely milled from the entire wheat kernel. Store white flour in an airtight container for 10 to 15 months; store wholemeal for up to 5 months. Flour may be refrigerated or frozen for longer storage.

ginger

The rhizome, or underground stem, of a semitropical plant, ginger is marketed fresh, dried, and ground into a powder, and as candied (glacé or crystallized) pieces preserved in a syrup and coated in sugar. Select fresh ginger roots that are firm, not shrivelled. Wrap in a paper towel and refrigerate for 2–3 weeks. Store ground and candied ginger for up to 6 months.

jams and preserves

Whether sandwiched between two cookie rounds, dropped in the middle of a chewy morsel, or swirled through rich bar cookie batter, jams and preserves add color and fruity flavor to cookies of all kinds. Be sure to use the best-quality spreads you can find, with true fruit flavor that isn't masked by too much sugar.

leaveners

Chemical leaveners cause cookies to rise as they bake. *Baking powder* reacts with liquid and/or heat to produce bubbles of carbon dioxide that cause batters and doughs to expand. When exposed to moisture and an acidic ingredient like buttermilk, yogurt, chocolate, or lemon juice, *baking soda (bicarbonate of soda)* also releases carbon dioxide gas. *Cream of tartar* is added to beaten egg whites as a stabilizer and is also mixed with commercial baking soda. Replace baking powder every 3 months.

nuts

Almonds, hazelnuts, macadamias, peanuts, pecans, pine nuts, pistachios, and walnuts add richness, texture, and flavor to cookie doughs and fillings. You'll find them in supermarkets packaged and in bulk in a number of forms, shelled and unshelled. Nuts are best used shortly after purchase; store in a cool, dry spot. Shelled nuts will keep longer if they are refrigerated or frozen in an airtight bag or container.

pumpkin

During the cool months, this winter vegetable finds its way into breads, cakes, pies, and cookies of all kinds, enhanced by spices such as cinnamon, nutmeg, ginger, cloves, and allspice.

raisins

These dried grapes are well-loved cookie additions. Every market sells them in boxes, packages, and in bulk. Dark seedless raisins have deep color and flavor, while golden seedless (sultanas) are pale and tangy. Dark and golden raisins are interchangeable in recipes, but raisins in an ingredients list usually means the former. Store unopened packages in a dry place; once opened, seal airtight and refrigerate or freeze.

rolled oats

When oats are steamed, then flattened by steel rollers into flakes, they are sold as rolled oats or old-fashioned oats. Quick-cooking oats and rolled oats can be used interchangeably. They add bulk, texture, and flavor to cookies. Store airtight for up to 6 months or freeze for up to 1 year.

spices

For centuries, spices like cinnamon, cloves, allspice, nutmeg, and ginger have added their distinctive character to baked goods. All spices are used in their dried form. Spices lose flavor after about 6 months if ground and after 2 years if whole. It is best to buy them whole in small quantities and grind them as needed, using a coffee grinder reserved solely for spices. Store in an airtight container (preferably glass) in a cool, dark, dry place.

sugars

These granular sweeteners add flavor and color to cookie doughs and batters, fillings, and frostings. *Dark brown sugar* (also known as *demerara sugar*) is a mixture of granulated sugar and molasses that adds rich, deep flavor. *Light brown sugar* has less molasses flavor than dark brown sugar. *Confectioners' sugar*, also called *icing sugar*, is ground and mixed with a small amount of cornstarch (cornflour) to prevent caking. Typically, it is used for frostings and coatings. *Granulated (white) sugar* is available in fine white crystals (most common) and superfine or caster (for frostings and meringues). Store any type of sugar indefinitely in airtight containers. Powdered artificial sweeteners cannot be substituted for sugar in baking.

sweeteners, liquid

Liquid sweeteners add their own character to cookies. Made by bees from floral nectar, *honey* is sweet and sticky and imparts rich flavor and perfume to batters, doughs, and fillings. It also enhances the keeping qualities of baked goods by retaining moisture and preventing them from becoming dry and stale. *Molasses* is a by-product of sugar-cane refining. *Light molasses (golden syrup)* is sweet and mild; *dark molasses (treacle)* is less sweet and more full-bodied. These two types of molasses are interchangeable in recipes. Unopened bottles of syrup last up to a year in a cool spot; after opening, store as directed on the label. Syrup and honey will pour off more freely from a measuring spoon or cup if either is first lightly oiled.

index

Page numbers in *italics* refer to photographs.

A

Afghans 72–3

Almond
  amaretti 238–9
  biscotti 246–7, *246–7*
  brittle 212
  cherry microwave
    cookies 224–5
  cookies 209–10
  cookies, Chinese 88–9
  cream 61
  crisps 218–19
  half-moons 244–5, *244–5*
  squares, apple and
    184–5
  strips, glazed 214–15
  tuiles 226–7

Amaretti 238–9

Anchovy and olive cookies
  276–7

Anise butterflies 116–17

Aniseed cookies 102–3

Anzac biscuits 96–7

Anzacs, walnut 254–5

Apple and almond squares
  184–5

Apricot
  cream cheese chocolate
    brownies 34–5
  crunch 164
  macaroon bars 174–5,
    174–5
  rugelach, white
    chocolate 66–7
  squares with yogurt
    topping, muesli- 196–7

B

Baking powder
  see Leaveners

Banana oaties 188–9

Bar cookies, making
  288–91

Basil oil 270

Berries with whipped
  cream 210

Berry cream 60

Biscotti
  almond 246–7, *246–7*
  chocolate hazelnut
    230–1, *246*
  spiced 232–3

Blonde brownies 51–2

Brandy sauce, microwave
  50

Brandy snaps with pastry
  cream 112–13, *112*

Brittle, nut 212–13
  almond 212
  date and peanut,
    microwave 213
  peanut brittle florentines
    216–17
  pecan, microwave 213

Brittle pieces 256, 308

Brownies
  apricot cream cheese
    chocolate 34–5
  blonde 51–2
  choc-coconut 198–9
  chocolate fudge,
    microwave 32–3

chocolate, with ice
    cream and chocolate
    sauce 56–7
chocolate raspberry 47–8
ginger 54–5
mocha 58–9
pecan fudge 38–9, *38–9*

Butter 267, 283

Butter brittle pieces 308

Butterflies, anise 116–17

Butterscotch sauce 53

Butters, herb 267

C

Caramel sauce 53

Caramel slice, microwave
    chocolate 30–1

Carrot raisin drops 168–9

Cheese cookies 272–3

Cheese, cream 167, 309

Cheese savories, Mexican
    262–3

Cheesecake dreams,
    orange 133–4

Cherry cookies 186–7

Chinese almond cookies
    88–9

Chinese stir-fry oil 271

Chips, pita 265

Chocolate 46, 301–2, 308
    apricot rugelach, white
        66–7
    brownies, apricot cream
        cheese 34–5
    brownies with ice cream
        and chocolate sauce
        56–7
    butter spritz 64–5
    caramel slice, microwave
        30–1
    -cherry parson's hats
        44–5, *44–5*
    chip cookies 11
    cream sauce 53
    -dipped mushrooms
        40–1, *40–1*
    double chocolate cookies
        14–15
    -drizzled praline cookies
        240–1, *240–1*
    fudge brownies
        microwave 32–3
        pecan 38–9, *38–9*
    hazelnut biscotti 230–1
    hazelnut cream 60

Kahlua truffle cookies
    22–3
madeleines 124–5,
    110–11
mint sandwich cookies
    20–1
nut cookies 16–17
peanut cookies 74–5
peppermint slices 26–7
pistachio sandwich
    cookies 42–3, *42–3*
raspberry brownies 47–8
salami 18–19
sauce 57
using/melting 46, 301–2,
    304–5, 308
wheaten cookies 70–1

Cinnamon crisps 78–9

Cinnamon snails 104–5,
    104–5

Citrus shortbread 144–5

Coconut 308
    and almond macaroons
        202–3
    and golden raisin cookies
        180–1, *180*
    choc-coconut brownies
        198–9
    macadamia cookies
        194–5

orange wafers 200–1
puffs 193
shortbread 86–7

Coffee 309
See also Mocha
cream icing 59
-pecan triangles 36–7,
37
walnut cookies 258

Cookies
making 280–305
packaging 306
storing 307

Crackers
pretzel 261
salt 268–9
water 274–5

Cream
berry 60
flavored 60–1
spiced whipped 61

Cream cheese 167, 309
chocolate brownies,
apricot 34–5
icing 167

Crunchy peanut cookies
252–3

Cutout cookies, making
292–3

D

Date
and oat slices 158–9
and peanut brittle 213
sticks 182
triangles, sour cream
165–6
and walnut cookies
250–1

Double chocolate cookies
14–15

Dough, cookie 280–5

Dried fruit 309, 311
See also by name of fruit
apricot crunch 164
apricot macaroon bars
174–5, *174–5*
carrot raisin drops 168–9
cherry cookies 186–7
coconut and golden
raisin cookies 180–1,
180–1
date and oat slices 158–9
date sticks 182
date triangles, sour
cream 165–6
date and walnut cookies
250–1
dried fruit cookies 151–2

eccles cakes 155
fruity foldovers 178–9,
178–9
muesli-apricot squares
with yogurt topping
196–7
nut and raisin squares
259
oatmeal and golden
raisin cookies 190–1
orange fig drops 172–3,
173
panforte 153–4
prune puffs 156–7
sour cream date triangles
165–6

Drop cookies
carrot raisin drops 168–9
making 286–7
orange fig drops 172–3,
173
peanut butter brittle
drops 256–7

E

Eccles cakes 155

Eggs 309

Espresso meringue kisses
12–13

F

Fats, cooking 309
  See also butter,
  margarine, oils

Florentines, peanut brittle
  216–17

Florentines, pecan 228–9

Flour 282, 285, 310

Frosted lime wafers 138–9

Fruit
  See also Dried fruit
  apple and almond
    squares 184–5
  apricot crunch 164
  banana oaties 188–9
  coconut and golden
    raisin cookies 180–1,
    180
  date and oat slices 158–9
  eccles cakes 155
  oatmeal and golden
    raisin cookies 190–1
  orange cheesecake
    dreams 133–4
  orange fig drops 172–3,
    173
  orange marmalade
    wreaths 146–7
  orange spice bars 149
  panforte 153–4
  sour cream date triangles
    165

Fruity foldovers 178–9,
  178–9

Fudge sauce, microwave
  50

G

Garlic butter 267

Garlic and lemon butter
  267

Ginger 310
  brownies 54–5
  crisps 126
  stars, molasses and 120–1

Gingerbread biscuits 80–1

Gingernuts 128–9

Glazed almond strips
  214–15

Golden raisin
  cookies, coconut and
    180–1, *180*
  cookies, oatmeal and
    190–1

Grissini, whole-grain 264

H

Hazelnut
  biscotti, chocolate 230–1
  macaroons 236–7
  toffee bars 205–6

Herb butters 267

Herb salt 266

Herbed oils 270–1

Holiday cookies 94–5

Honey snowflakes 98–9

I

Ice cream sandwiches 62–3

Icing
  coffee cream 59
  cream cheese 167
  orange liqueur 183
  rum and ginger 183
  using/making 303, 304–5

J, K

Jams and preserves 310

Kahlua coffee liqueur 18,
  19, 22–3

Koulourakia 90–1

L

Ladyfingers 118–19

Leaveners 310

Lemon butter, microwave 148

Lemon cream cheese icing 167

Lemon-ginger tea cookies 140–1

Lemon-pistachio pretzels 142–3

Lemon thins, meringue-topped 136–7

Lime wafers, frosted 138–9

Linzer sandwich rings 242–3, *242–3*

M

Macaroon bars, apricot 174–5, *174–5*

Macaroons, coconut and almond 202–3

Macaroons, hazelnut 236–7

Madeleines 110–11, *110*

chocolate *110, 124–5*
spiced 122–3

Margarine 283

Marmalade wreaths, orange 146–7

Marshmallow sandwich cookies 24–5

Mediterranean herb oil 271

Melting moments 92–3

Meringue kisses, espresso 12–13

Meringues, making 302–3

Meringue-topped lemon thins 136–7

Mexican cheese savories 262–3

Mexican peanut cookies 207–8

Microwave cooking 28–9
almond cherry cookies 224–5
chocolate caramel slice 30–1
chocolate fudge brownies 32–3
date and peanut brittle 213

lemon butter 148
orange sauce 135
pear and ginger sauce 55
pecan brittle 213
sauces 50, 55, 135

Mixed herb butter 267

Mocha brownies 58–9

Mocha shortbread 84–5

Mocha tea cookies 68–9

Molasses and ginger stars 120–1

Molasses spice cookies 127

Muesli-apricot squares with yogurt topping 196–7

N

Nut brittles 212–13

Nut cookies, chocolate 16–17

Nut and raisin squares 259

Nuts 310–11
See also by name of nut

Nuts, using 211, 305

O

Oatmeal and golden raisin cookies 190–1

Oats, rolled 311

Oils, herbed 270–1

Olive cookies, anchovy and 276–7

Orange
cheesecake dreams 133–4
fig drops 172–3, *173*
liqueur icing 183
marmalade wreaths 146–7
spice bars 149

P

Packaging ideas 306

Panforte 153–4

Parsley butter 267

Party ideas 305

Peanut butter bonbons 222–3

Peanut butter brittle drops 256–7

Peanut
brittle, date and 213
brittle florentines 216–17
cookies, chocolate 74–5
cookies, crunchy 252–3
cookies, Mexican 207–8

Pear and ginger sauce, microwave 55

Pecan
brittle, microwave 213
florentines 228–9
fudge brownies 38–9, *38–9*
shortbread 82–3, *108*
triangles, coffee- 36–7, *37*

Peppermint slices, chocolate 26–7

Pine nut cookies 220–1

Pirouettes, chocolate-dipped *see* Almond crisps

Pistachio pretzels, lemon- 142–3

Pistachio sandwich cookies, chocolate 42–3, *42–3*

Pita chips 265

Polvorones 234–5

Praline cookies, chocolate-drizzled 240–1, *241*

Pressed (spritz) cookies, making 298–9

Pretzel crackers 261

Pretzels, lemon-pistachio 142–3

Pretzels, shaping 297

Prune puffs 156–7

Pumpkin 311
spice bars 170–1
swirls 162–3

R

Raisins 311
See also dried fruit

Raspberry
brownies, chocolate 47–8
-orange strips 176–7, *176*
pinwheels 106–7, *106–7*
sauce 49

Ricotta foldovers 160–1

Rugelach, white chocolate
    apricot 66–7

Rum and spice cookies
    114–15

S

Salt crackers 268–9

Sandwich cookies
    chocolate mint 20–1
    chocolate pistachio
        42–3, *42–3*
    marshmallow 24–5

Sandwich rings, Linzer
    242–3, *242–3*

Sauce
    brandy, microwave 50
    butterscotch 53
    caramel 53
    chocolate 57
    chocolate cream 53
    fudge, microwave 50
    orange, microwave 135
    pear and ginger,
        microwave 55
    raspberry 49

Savories, Mexican cheese
    262–3

Savory cookies 261–77
    anchovy and olive 276–7
    cheese 272–3
    Mexican cheese savories
        262–3
    pita chips 265
    pretzel crackers 261
    salt crackers 268–9
    water crackers 275
    whole-grain grissini 264

Sesame fork cookies
    248–9, *248*

Shaped and molded
    cookies, making 296–7

Shortbread 108–9, *108–9*
    citrus 144–5
    coconut 86–7
    mocha 84–5
    pecan 82–3, *109*

Shortening 283
    See also butter, fats,
        margarine, oils

Sliced cookies, making
    294–5

Sour cream date triangles
    165–6

Spice bars, orange 149

Spice bars, pumpkin 170–1

Spice cookies 100–1
    molasses and 127
    rum and 114–15

Spiced biscotti 232–3

Spiced madeleines 122–3

Spiced whipped cream 61

Spices 311

Spritz, chocolate butter
    64–5

Spritz (pressed) cookies,
    making 298–9

Storage of cookies 307

Sugar 282–3, 312
    See also sweeteners

Sugar cookies 77

Sugar-glazed vanilla
    cookies 130–1

Sweeteners 312
    See also Sugar

T

Tea cookies,
    lemon-ginger 140–1

Tea cookies, mocha 68–9

Toffee bars, hazelnut
    205–6

Toppings and meringues
    300–3

Truffle cookies,
    chocolate Kahlua 22–3

V

Vanilla cookies, sugar
    glazed 130–1

Vanilla cream 61

W

Walnut anzacs 254–5

Walnut cookies, coffee
    258

Walnut cookies, date
    and 250–1

Water crackers 274–5

White chocolate apricot
    rugelach 66–7

Whole-grain grissini 264

a note on
measurements

U.S. cup measurements are
used throughout this book.
Slight adjustments may
need to be made to
quantities if Imperial or
metric measures are used.

....

acknowledgments

Weldon Owen wishes to
thank the following people
for their help in producing
this book: Ad-Libitum/Stuart
Bowey (cover photography);
Nancy Sibtain (index); Sarah
Anderson, Tracey Gibson,
Kylie Mulquin, and Marney
Richardson (testing recipes).

biscottislice
shortbread
snapsbonbo
tuilespinwh
cookieswaf
biscuitspre